YOU CAN

FOR AGES
7-11

"Thinking skills are a powerful means of improving the quality of learning in classrooms."

DfES

Author
Sue Cowley

Editor
Sara Wiegand

Assistant Editor
Catherine Gilhooly

Illustrations
Mike Phillips

Series Designer
Catherine Mason

Designer
Helen Taylor

Cover concept/designer
Anna Oliwa

Cover illustration
© stockbyte/punchstock

Text © 2006 Sue Cowley

© 2006 Scholastic Ltd

Designed using Adobe InDesign

Published by Scholastic Ltd
Villiers House
Clarendon Avenue
Leamington Spa
Warwickshire CV32 5PR

www.scholastic.co.uk

Printed by Bell and Bain Ltd.
4 5 6 7 8 9   8 9 0 1 2 3 4

British Library Cataloguing-in-Publication Data
A catalogue record for this book is available from the British Library.
ISBN 0-439-96555-1
ISBN 978-0439-96555-2

The rights of the author Sue Cowley have been asserted in accordance with the Copyright, Designs and Patents Act 1988.

Contents

Contents

Introduction

In recent years there has been increased interest in the ways children learn and the kind of skills we should be teaching them. More and more, we are being encouraged to think about how children learn, rather than simply about which facts or skills we wish to teach them. Teachers have many demands on their time – keeping up with changes to the curriculum, completing paperwork, planning for literacy – all on top of their actual classroom practice. You might feel that you have little space or energy left to deliver yet another set of skills. But the development of thinking is not something to 'add on' to what we already do, it is a fundamental aspect of learning.

Cross-curricular benefits

Thinking skills help with learning in all areas of the curriculum. A single skill, such as lateral thinking, has applications across subject areas. Each part of the curriculum uses its own special thinking techniques, but these methods aid learning whatever the subject material. Using symbolism in English will help your children explore religious festivals; studying digestion in science will show your children the importance of healthy eating.

Joined-up thinking

After years of the curriculum being divided into ever-smaller chunks, the pendulum is swinging back in the other direction. At last we are being asked to see the subjects as linked and interrelated. This mirrors the ways our brains work: by making connections and seeing how apparently unrelated areas might join up together. A thinking approach to learning will show your children the connections between different curriculum areas: how art relates to maths, how drama and history are connected.

Building concentration

These days, children have many demands on their time and attention. If your pupils lack concentration, this can really interfere with the day-to-day running of your classroom. Misbehaviour, or a lack of focus, can undermine the learning of the entire class. The development of thinking skills will really benefit your children's concentration. It shows them strategies for working in a thoughtful, intelligent way, and this can be of particular benefit for your less able pupils.

The thoughtful teacher

Finally, the exercises and activities which develop thinking skills are often a great deal of fun for the teacher to deliver. Taking a thinking approach to your work will encourage you to be imaginative and experimental, and to keep your teaching fresh and innovative.

You can... Make the most of group work

Group work is a great way of developing thinking skills. This format allows the children to share ideas, to bounce thoughts off each other, and also to learn how to work cooperatively.

Thinking points

● Although group work is useful for developing thinking skills, it can be tricky to manage effectively. This is where the management skills of the teacher come into play.

● One of the main difficulties with groups is keeping the children on task. Having a continuous process of feedback during activities will help keep the groups focused on the work.

● Given the choice, your children will group themselves with their friends. This can work well, but will often lead to excessive social chat rather than work.

Tips, ideas and activities

● Think about appropriate groupings for different tasks, using a range of approaches to create groups. For example:

● Random groupings
Try using a numbering system. Decide how many pupils you want in each group (such as four). Divide the total number in the class by this amount (24 ÷ 4 = 6 groups). The children count around the room up to this number. All of the 'One's' work together, all the 'Two's' and so on.

● Mixed ability groupings
The more able pupils will often extend their less able classmates. Watch that one really bright child does not end up 'running' the group. Remember that academic ability does not necessarily correlate to good speaking and listening skills.

● Same ability groupings
Children can feel more confident about contributing when they are working at the same level as the others in the group.

● Groupings with set roles
Give each child in the group a specific role to fulfil (for example, group leader, note-taker, maverick and so on).

● Thinking hats groupings
The Thinking hats idea, devised by Edward de Bono (see www.edwdebono.com), will help your children take a range of perspectives in their thinking. The 'hats' come in different colours to denote the kind of thinking taking place; white for facts, green for creative, and so on.

● Consider the timing of group exercises. Too much time and your pupils are likely to go off-task. Often a short time frame will create a positive focus and energy within groups.

● Ask pupils to think about how they approach group tasks. Can they choose an animal which best describes their style?

● A mouse; keeps quiet, listens to what others have to say.

● A lion; takes control, makes others listen to their ideas.

● An elephant; slow to take part but a 'heavyweight' within the group.

● An owl; wise, making contributions, but taking other ideas on board.

You can... Use questions to develop thinking

Questions form a crucial part of every teacher's classroom technique, especially when it comes to developing thinking skills. Although it might appear a simple thing to do, making effective use of questions is actually much harder than you might think.

Thinking points

● Children learn the word 'why' early on and go on to drive their parents mad with it! It's a great tool for them to learn about the world.

● Just as with other areas of classroom management, it pays to have clear rules and high expectations for question and answer sessions.

● Encourage your pupils to ask questions themselves, rather than viewing them as the sole province of the teacher.

● Remember that questions don't always have to be used with the whole class. You can develop lots of thinking by using them during group work as well.

● Bear in mind that open questions will use up more lesson time than the more straightforward closed ones, so leave plenty of time when using this approach.

Tips, ideas and activities

● Think about your use of questions and try to achieve a good balance between the different types. For example:

○ Closed questions
What is 8 x 3? Is Paris the capital of France? These questions require a 'yes' or 'no' answer, or a simple one-word response. The teacher already has an answer in mind and the children must respond in a predetermined way. These questions are useful for assessing an understanding or retention of facts. However, they do little to develop independent thinking. Watch that you don't rely too heavily on this type of question.

○ Open questions
What is your favourite food and why? What are your views on hunting? These questions invite a whole range of potential responses, with no one 'right' answer. This type of question is excellent for developing thinking skills, as it encourages a more detailed, personal and creative response.

○ Rhetorical questions
What on earth are you doing? Why are you messing around again? We often use these questions in connection with misbehaviour. Make sure you don't use too many rhetorical questions – it's a habit that we get into without realising. Try only to ask a question if you actually want an answer.

● In whole class question sessions, don't always pick on volunteers with their hands up to answer. This can mean the quiet children (and the lazy ones) never get to contribute. Be sensitive and avoid putting children on the spot. Give the class some 'thinking time' before asking individuals, or give the option to 'pass' if a pupil is really stuck. Here are a few alternatives:

○ Everyone answers; the pupils all shout out their answers simultaneously.

○ Tell your neighbour; the children tell the person sitting next to them.

○ Luck of the draw; place a playing card on each seat, and ask for an answer from the child holding the Ace of Spades, the Four of Hearts and so on.

You Can... **Think about your use of space**

The way that we use our teaching spaces has a significant impact on the type and quality of the thinking done within a particular space. Analyse your personal use of space, or look at the way you set up your classroom, to help you develop thinking skills.

Thinking points

● Although habit and routine are very useful for classroom management, they tend to work against creative and original thought.

● Teachers can get into habits with their teaching styles, particularly when it comes to their use of the classroom space.

● Keeping your use of space fresh and imaginative will help you keep your pupils 'on their toes'; they never know quite what to expect from you.

● Being innovative with space will encourage your children to take new perspectives on their work, and to develop their thinking in more original ways.

Tips, ideas and activities

● Consider your teaching position; where you stand in relation to your pupils. Do you tend to stay at the front of the room, stuck in the same location? Try teaching from different places in the classroom, for example:

- Talk to the class from the back of the room. Ask the pupils to stay facing the front and not to turn to face you, listening only to your voice. This will force them to listen more carefully, because they cannot get any non-verbal cues from your face or body.
- Sit with the children in a circle on the floor to read them a story. Ask them to close their eyes and to visualise the story in their heads.
- Sit on a desk in a relaxed posture to encourage more informal thinking from your children.
- Crouch down beside a child to tease out some individual ideas.

● Think about the way your classroom is laid out and whether this layout helps or hinders the development of thinking skills. Don't be afraid to change the layout, perhaps asking the pupils to move the desks for a particular lesson, or adapting your classroom layout once every couple of weeks. As a general rule of thumb:

- Desks laid out in rows are good for managing behaviour and for individual question and answer sessions.
- Desks set up in groups are useful for activities which involve pupil discussions and small group thinking.
- Desks in a 'U' shape are effective for holding debates and for encouraging the children to share thoughts with each other, as well as with the teacher.
- Chairs in a circle are good for activities needing equal participation from all members of the class.
- No desks at all is a good format for active, practical work. This format tends to encourage creative thinking and can free up the imagination.

You Can... Use your voice to encourage thinking

Your use of voice can improve the quality of the learning that takes place in your classroom. Your pupils spend a lot of their time listening to you speak; think about how you might improve this aspect of your teaching.

Thinking points

● Learning to use your voice properly is essential, because in the classroom you spend all day, every day speaking.

● Incorrect voice usage can lead to problems with sore throats, lost voices, and even to long-term damage.

● Teachers will often talk more than is strictly necessary. Learn to curb this impulse in yourself, letting the children take over the learning whenever possible.

● Where a teacher's voice is difficult to understand, this can lead to misbehaviour because the children do not focus on what is being said.

Tips, ideas and activities

● Tape yourself teaching to find out how your voice sounds to your children. Listen to the tape and consider:
  ● How much of the time do you spend speaking?
  ● What do you say and how does this help to develop your pupils' thinking?
  ● Do you talk with a range of children, or do some pupils get more of your verbal input than others?
  ● Is your voice always clear, easily understood and pitched at an appropriate volume?
  ● How interesting is your vocal sound? Could you listen to yourself all day?
  ● Is the vocabulary you use sometimes too complicated or too simple?
  ● Does your voice give away your emotions? For example, stress caused by difficult behaviour?
  ● How often do you shout? What are the effects of raising your voice on the class?

● Make use of different vocal speeds to engage the children. You could:
  ● Speak with a fast pace to create an air of excitement and interest.
  ● Speak slowly when you have something tricky to explain.
  ● Incorporate pauses into your speaking, particularly during question and answer sessions, giving the pupils space to think.

● Think about your use of tone and how you can adapt it to develop thinking. For example, using a curious tone when asking questions, or putting a stress on key words and points when introducing a new topic.

● Let your pupils hear other people speaking. This gives them a break from your voice and encourages them to listen more carefully. To find these 'other voices' you could:
  ● Ask a teaching assistant to read a story to the class.
  ● Invite a parent in to talk to the class about his or her work.
  ● Do some team teaching with a teacher from another class.
  ● Play tapes or CDs to the children.
  ● If you can, put on a different accent to talk to the class.

You Can... **Try some experimental teaching**

Teachers can feel weighed down by curriculum demands and have the sense that they must not be seen to 'fail'. However, creative thinking will often happen when you try an unusual activity; one that has the potential to go wrong.

Thinking points

● However hard, try not to let outside pressures turn you into a teacher who always plays it safe. Being experimental or original in your teaching can lead to some really inspirational lessons. It's also a great deal of fun!

● The more experienced you are as a classroom manager, the more comfortable you will feel in taking some risks in your teaching. If you are new to teaching, wait until the second or third term, when your class are settled and closely controlled.

● Teaching an experimental lesson does not mean a 'free-for-all' for the children. In fact, this kind of lesson will often require far more self-discipline than the more straightforward, structured ones.

Tips, ideas and activities

● Use props to inspire your children's curiosity and jolt them into some imaginative thinking. For example:
  ● A bag or suitcase, filled with some unusual items. Ask the class what kind of person owns the bag, or encourage them to devise a story about the journeys that the suitcase has been on.
  ● A locked treasure chest. Encourage the children to think about what they should do with it. How can they open it? Should they leave it shut?
  ● Some archaeological artefacts. For the best results, bury your objects in the school grounds, so that the children can 'discover' them.

● Try some lessons where you turn your teaching space into a completely different place or setting. You could:
  ● Set up your classroom as a damaged spaceship, turning over desks and chairs to help simulate the interior of the ship.
  ● Get the children to act as sick and injured astronauts. For extra interest and realism, allow them to use face paints to draw on their injuries.
  ● Ask for two volunteers to 'beam down' onto the spaceship, to see what has happened.
  ● If possible, add atmosphere by darkening the room and giving the pupils torches.
  ● Ask the visiting astronauts to devise a story as they look around, by talking about what they see.
  ● Perhaps they are concerned that the ship has been caught in a black hole? Maybe they are worried that aliens are on board? Perhaps they think that the astronauts have a deadly virus?

● When teaching new concepts, use concrete examples to bring them to life. This will help you to find more innovative ways of teaching. For example, to explain how adverbs enhance writing, you could:
  ● Invite a pupil to demonstrate a verb (for example, swim).
  ● Ask the rest of the class to think of ideas and suggest adverbs.
  ● With each new adverb, your volunteer must change his or her swimming action accordingly (for example, slowly, manically, clumsily).

You Can... Get your children thinking about behaviour

We cannot force our children to behave; we can only explain their choices and help them understand the consequences of making the wrong decision. Get your pupils to think about their behaviour and hopefully they will learn to behave better.

Thinking points

● When it comes to dealing with behaviour, never lose sight of the fact that 'children will be children'. Try not to focus too much on the minor irritations or the silly, childish behaviour that is essentially harmless.

● If you can encourage your children to have a greater sense of empathy, they will better understand how their behaviour impacts on others.

● Give your pupils a choice when it comes to behaviour; this helps to depersonalise the giving of sanctions. Either they choose to follow the rules, or they should accept the punishment for breaking them with good grace.

● Where rules and standards are realistic, and we have played a part in devising them, we are far more likely to stick to them. This applies as much to teachers using a school behaviour policy as it does to children following a set of class rules.

Tips, ideas and activities

● Get your children involved in creating your class rules. Ask them to think about:
  ○ Why do we need rules in society and in school?
  ○ What rules do they want for their classroom?
  ○ What sanctions are appropriate for pupils breaking these rules?
  ○ What rewards would work for children who follow the rules?

● Do some exercises on building empathy and on 'reading' people's emotional state by looking at facial expressions and body language. (This skill is often under-developed in poorly behaved children.) You could:
  ○ Show the class pictures of people in different emotional states. (Cut these out of magazines, or use photographs of family and friends.) Ask the children: *How are these people feeling? How can you tell?*
  ○ Explain that you are going to enter the room in a specific mood, but that you are not going to say anything. Ask them to guess your mood, simply by looking at you. Leave the room and enter in a variety of moods: angry, sad, happy, excited and so on. Discuss how they could tell your feelings through your face and body language.

● Drama offers a great way to improve understanding of human behaviour. This activity will help your children understand how their behaviour impacts on you and your teaching.
  ○ Ask a volunteer to play the teacher, perhaps a child who is quite disruptive.
  ○ Explain that he or she has the same authority and rights as a teacher (such as giving sanctions and rewards).
  ○ Give the child a simple task to complete, for example pretending to take the register.
  ○ Explain that you are going to play a 'naughty child'.
  ○ As the pupil takes the register, begin to misbehave. Be as disruptive and defiant as you like!
  ○ When you have finished, ask the 'teacher' and the class how your behaviour made them feel.

You Can... **Build your children's powers of observation**

The ability to pay close attention to something or someone plays a key part in effective learning. Being able to observe well and closely will help your children in many areas of the curriculum, for example Art, English and Science.

Thinking points

- A key factor in effective observation is being able to use the skills of focus and concentration.

- Building better observational skills with your children will help increase their ability to concentrate.

- We might think that we are good at accurate observation. Often, though, we will see or remember what we imagine is there, rather than what is actually there.

Tips, ideas and activities

- Play the game 'Who's missing?' This is a good activity for a new class to learn faces and names. It is also effective for testing observational skills.
  - Ask for a volunteer to work out 'Who's missing?'
  - This child stands up and closes his or her eyes.
  - Now ask for a volunteer to 'go missing'.
  - Pick a child by pointing at them (don't say anything). This child steps outside.
  - 'Shuffle' the rest of the class, so that they sit in a different seat.
  - The volunteer opens his or her eyes and works out 'Who's missing?'
  - Adapt the above to play a game of 'What's missing?' During a break, remove one object from your classroom. When the children come back in, ask them to work out 'What's missing?' It is not necessarily the small items that are hardest to spot. Try removing something really big, for example a piece of furniture; often when we are very familiar with something, we overlook it.

- Try this 'eyewitness' activity, using the photocopiable sheet on page 56 ('Eyewitness account'). This is a fun exercise to get your pupils using their powers of observation. It is also a good way of exploring how eyewitness accounts might differ, an important historical skill.
  - Arrange for a colleague to help you, preferably someone the children don't know well.
  - During a lesson, ask this person to run into your classroom and do something surprising, then to run out again. For example, the person could run in and grab an item from your classroom and pretend to steal it.
  - Now ask the children to complete their 'Eyewitness account'.
  - Share their accounts, looking at how and why the versions differ.
  - Bring your colleague back into the room to check the accuracy of the children's accounts.

You Can... **Help your pupils use metacognition**

The better your pupils understand their thought processes, the more they will be able to extend their thinking. A clearer understanding of how their brains work will help your children develop their own strategies for learning.

Thinking points

● The term 'metacognition' describes the way we can think about our own thinking; having an awareness of what happens in our minds when we think about something.

● Exploring what goes on in our brains when we think is useful for developing better approaches to learning. It is also fascinating in its own right.

● Using metacognition helps your children understand how they as individuals learn best. It can help them recognise their own preferred learning styles, and consequently to create personal learning strategies for different activities.

● The way we think depends on the task we are doing. Our primary way of thinking typically involves language; silently turning over different thoughts in our minds.

● Some people take more visual approaches to thinking than others. Encourage your pupils to think using images, colours, and so on, as well as words.

Tips, ideas and activities

● Split your class into groups. Give each group a jigsaw puzzle in a see-through bag. Have the pictures of each completed puzzle available (either on the box or as a photocopy of the completed jigsaw), but do not give the pictures to the children.

● Ask a series of questions to encourage metacognition, giving the groups a short discussion time for each one. Ask the children to *think first* and not to touch the puzzle until you say.

  ● What comes into your mind when you see the jigsaw?
  ● What is the first thing you would do when you get the puzzle out of the bag?
  ● Do different people in your group have different ideas about what to do first?
  ● Why is this? Which idea do you think will work best?
  ● What is the next step you are going to take and why?
  ● Are there a variety of ideas in your group about what to do?
  ● Is there anything that I could give you that would make it easier for you to solve the puzzle?

● Now hand out the pictures that go with each puzzle. Ask the pupils to talk about what happens in their minds when they first see the picture of the completed jigsaw.

● Finish the activity by asking the children to complete their puzzles. You could set a challenge to see which group can finish first.

● When the jigsaws have been done, talk with your class about the exercise. Explain the term 'metacognition' to the children and ask them to describe their awareness of their own thought processes during the jigsaw activity.

● As an extension, you might ask the pupils to describe their thoughts during this exercise by:
  ● creating a symbolic picture or a collage
  ● devising a piece of percussive music
  ● using a series of movements or frozen poses.

You Can... Develop your children's listening skills

For effective learning to take place your children must develop the ability to listen well. Good quality listening skills play a key role in the development of thinking, because they give us access to the thoughts, ideas and knowledge of others.

Thinking points

● Some children will appear to be good listeners, simply because they are silent and apparently paying attention. It is vital to ensure that they do actually understand what is being said.

● You can do this by getting continual feedback from the class during spoken sessions. This feedback might involve questioning the pupils, or asking them to summarise what has been said.

● Some children find it really hard to assimilate spoken information and quickly switch off. To maintain good focus do not talk at your class for extended periods of time.

● For group work to be successful, the children must learn to listen to each other, as well as to the teacher.

Tips, ideas and activities

● Ask your children to think about what happens in their heads as they listen to different stimuli, for example a story, a piece of music or a prayer.

● Play some games that rely on the use of listening skills. For example, traditional games:
  - Chinese whispers
  - 20 questions
  - Port/starboard
  - Simon says…

● Create variations on the above to keep them interesting, for example:
  - 'Put your', a variation of 'Simon says'. The children follow a series of spoken commands, involving body parts and left/right. For example, 'Put your left hand on your right knee; Put your right thumb on your head'.
  - 'All mixed up', as above but in pairs. The two players connect the body parts with each other, keeping each part in contact until they are all twisted up!

● Place a picture on an easel at the front of the classroom, positioned so that the children cannot see it. Invite a volunteer to describe the picture to the rest of class and ask the children to draw it from this spoken description.

● Set listening challenges to make everyday tasks more interesting. For example, when taking the register, ask the children to spot a name of a child who is not in the class. The first to spot the deliberate mistake gets a reward.

● Your children will get used to the sound of your voice and it can be really helpful for them to hear other accents, genders and so on. Play your children a CD or tape of a poem or story, without any accompanying text. Listen several times through, setting a different focus each time. Ask them to listen:
  - for pleasure, with no particular purpose
  - for a general overview of meaning
  - for a specific word, perhaps counting how many times it occurs
  - for tone and emotion in the speaker's voice.

You Can... **Help your children to use memory strategies**

As with any other skill, we can improve and increase our ability to remember things by learning some simple strategies. Having a better memory will help your children in areas such as spelling and the retention of facts and information.

Thinking points

● In order to improve our memories, we need to be aware of how the brain works when we think.

● As we grow and experience the world, the cells within our brains link up together. A network of pathways is created so that electrical impulses can pass from one cell (or neuron) to another.

● We remember things best when we mimic this linking process, by making connections between things.

● Negative experiences will often stick in our memories far more strongly than more positive ones, for example a disgusting taste or a bad experience from our own school days.

Tips, ideas and activities

● In groups, ask your children to talk about memory, discussing:
  - Their earliest memory, encouraging them to describe this in as much detail as possible.
  - Why they have remembered this particular event.
  - Whether there are any similarities between the first memories of different group members.
  - How their brains make these particular events 'stick' in their minds.

● Explore some mnemonics with your class (a system that helps you to remember something, often using memorable words and phrases). Think about how and why this approach works. Look at www.eudesign.com/mnems/ for some great suggestions. Here are some classic mnemonics that you might remember from your own childhood:
  - '**N**ever **E**at **S**hredded **W**heat'; for remembering the order of the points on the compass (**N**orth, **E**ast, **S**outh, **W**est).
  - '**R**ichard **O**f **Y**ork **G**ave **B**attle **I**n **V**ain'; for remembering the order of the colours of the rainbow (**r**ed, **o**range, **y**ellow, **g**reen, **b**lue, **i**ndigo, **v**iolet).
  - 'I before E, except after C'; for remembering how to spell words that have 'ie' in them.
  - **B**ig **e**lephants **c**an **a**dd **u**p **s**ums **e**asily; for remembering how to spell 'because'.

● Examine the key role of our senses in remembering. Ask the children to think about each of their senses in turn, and to consider which ones provide the most vivid memories. Perhaps surprisingly, smell often brings up the most powerful memories, the slightest scent taking us instantly back to a place or time from the past.

● Teach your children a simple number memory system:
  - Pick a rhyming word for each number, from one to five. For example, link 'one' with 'sun', 'two' with 'shoe' and so on.
  - Choose five things to remember, for example five objects around the classroom.
  - Teach the children to create links between their number words and the objects, by creating vivid mental images connecting the two. For example, to remember 'window', create a mental picture of a really hot sun burning through the window on a summer's day.

You Can... Develop lateral and creative thoughts

Much of the thinking that takes place in the classroom is fairly straightforward, often requiring the application of logic or analysis. The ability to use lateral thought will give your children access to more original, unusual and innovative ideas.

Thinking points

● The brain works by searching for recognisable patterns to find meaning. Even though a house and a tower block are very different, we can still understand that they are both types of buildings with things in common.

● Our thinking process often tends to follow straight lines, with one thought or idea leading to the next.

● When we use lateral thinking, we aim to break away from looking for typical patterns and a single line of thought.

● This type of original thought does not always sit well within the standardised curriculum we are asked to teach. However, it is highly prized in the world beyond school.

Tips, ideas and activities

● Talk with your pupils about what lateral thinking is. Help them understand this concept by using the example of a journey. To drive from home to school, we would normally take the most direct route. However, if we come up against an obstacle (for example, road works), we have to divert down a side road to get to our destination. This taking of an unusual diversion is what lateral thinking is like.

● Give the class some suggestions to help them take these 'side roads' in their thinking. For example, they could:

　● Turn their thinking upside down so that they come at a problem, question or puzzle from the opposite direction. For example, deciding to leave the car behind and walk around the road works.

　● Reinterpret the original question, so that it has a different sense or meaning.

　● Do the opposite of normal, logical thinking and try out some mad or silly ideas instead.

　● Swap the perspective so that they look at an issue from another angle, for example talking with the workmen and asking if they would mind letting you through.

● Set up a series of 'impossible' problems for your children to solve; keep your instructions deliberately vague and ambiguous. This will push the pupils into using lateral and creative thought. Engage in lots of talking and thinking about possible approaches, encouraging the children to experiment with solutions in small groups and as a whole class. For example:

　● Take the class into a large open space. Create two 'islands' at opposite ends of the space, by putting large sheets of paper or big cloths on the floor. Divide the children into groups and ask them to cross the space between the two islands without touching the ground.

　● Find a book written in another language. Show it to the class and ask for volunteers to read it.

　● Show the children a locked box. Tell them that they must open it without touching it.

　● Give a pack of cards to each group and ask them to create a structure that reaches the classroom ceiling.

You Can... **Use structures to develop thinking**

Although thought takes place in the mind, we can use written structures to help us develop our thinking further and to record the ideas that we have. These structures will help your children generate, organise and retain ideas and information.

Thinking points

● The best structures for developing thought are those which mirror the way that our brains work.

● This is why spidergrams and mind maps are so effective; they mirror the network of pathways that is formed in the brain as we think.

● Spidergrams are a very popular structure for learning; they offer an ideal method for gathering lots of ideas together at the start of a lesson or topic. This format also provides an ideal way to plan essays and revise for exams.

● The mind map, invented by Tony Buzan, offers a way of extending the classic spidergram. This structure uses diagrams, colours, symbols, and so on, to create a larger web of thought.

Tips, ideas and activities

● Talk with your pupils about the differences between a spidergram and a mind map. For example a mind map:
  ● is larger and more complex
  ● contains related ideas around a large subject area
  ● has several layers of connections (for example, not just one set of points connected to the central idea, as in a typical spidergram)
  ● uses a range of diagrammatic symbols; lines, arrows, circles, and so on
  ● uses colours to differentiate between various kinds of ideas
  ● uses images to help clarify meaning.

● Show your class examples of mind maps. Look on the website www.mind-mapping.co.uk

● Create a whole-class mind map. Choose a subject that involves thinking across a range of related areas, for example the science topic, 'Staying healthy'.
  ● Divide the class into small groups.
  ● Give each group a different area to think about and research.
  ● In this topic, you could use healthy foods, unhealthy foods, exercise, the healthy body, heart and pulse rate, harmful substances and so on.
  ● Ask each group to produce a detailed diagram on one area, to include several layers of ideas, colours, symbols, images and so on. This should be presented on a large sheet of paper (A2 or bigger).
  ● Invite each group to give a short presentation to the class, explaining their thinking.
  ● Take the class to an open space, for example the hall.
  ● Lay the diagrams on the floor, in a large circle. Rotate the groups around the circle to study each diagram in turn.
  ● Ask the children to find connections between their own diagram and the ideas in the others, making a note of these connections and considering what creates them.
  ● For example, 'cholesterol' under 'unhealthy foods' links to 'heart disease' under 'heart', with 'blocked arteries' creating the link.
  ● Tape the mind maps together. Ask volunteers to draw arrows showing the links, writing the connecting ideas along the arrows.

You Can... **Use the senses to enhance thinking**

We use our senses to interact with and literally make sense of the world around us. Although we might use our senses primarily to gather information, we can also use them to stimulate and inspire creative, imaginative thought.

Thinking points
● For a large majority of their time in school, your children will be making most use of their sight and hearing.

● Find ways to incorporate their other senses into lessons. This will add interest and excitement to lessons and encourage your pupils to think more widely.

● Taking away one sense (for instance, by blindfolding a child) will make the other senses more responsive.

● It will also give your children an insight into how people with sensory impairment experience the world.

Tips, ideas and activities
● Use the photocopiable sheet on page 57 ('The senses'). This exercise helps your children to develop their thinking by using all of their senses.

● Collect a wide range of sensory materials, for example:
  ○ Hearing: musical instruments, glass jars filled with beans or pebbles, glasses filled with water (make a sound by rubbing a finger around the rim).
  ○ Touch: natural objects (such as stones, bark, leaves and twigs), velvet, leather, clingfilm, tin foil, plasticine, clay.
  ○ Taste: a range of foods and drinks (avoid anything that might cause an allergic reaction).
  ○ Smell: distinctive fruits such as lemon and banana, washing powder, coffee, metal.

● Keep the resources hidden; use a large bag for each set of objects, or cover them up with a cloth.

● Find some blindfolds or make simple ones out of scarves or pieces of material. Have one blindfold for each pair of children.

● Divide your pupils into pairs; one person wears the blindfold, the other fills out the sheet.

● Once the children are blindfolded, hand out the first selection of materials. You could have all the children working with one sense (such as hearing) at the same time, or have them working with different senses.

● When the sheet has been completed, encourage the children to talk through their findings. Ask:
  ○ Did you find it easy to identify all the objects?
  ○ Was there one sense that worked particularly well?
  ○ Which objects provoked the strongest associations?

● Swap the pairs over and repeat the exercise.

● Develop some cross-curricular work out of this exercise, for example:
  ○ Science: exploring how our senses work.
  ○ Creative writing: using the associations as a starting point for a poem.
  ○ Art: drawing a smell or a taste.
  ○ Maths: sort materials into different types by touch.

You Can... Incorporate a range of learning styles

Even though there is controversy about the scientific basis behind 'learning styles', it is obvious that different children do prefer to learn in different ways. Using a range of approaches in lessons will help interest and engage all of your children.

Thinking points

● Consider how you think and how this changes according to the activity. A lot of the time we think in words, but for some activities we might think in pictures, numbers and so on.

● Often, the learning done at school requires children to look and listen. Some pupils will find this particularly hard and will respond much better to taking active approaches to their work.

● It is almost impossible to differentiate for the different learning styles of each pupil; what you can do is incorporate a range of methods in each lesson.

Tips, ideas and activities

● Here are some thoughts about adding sound and auditory interest to your teaching.

  ● Incorporate music into your teaching; as a way of starting the day, or as part of the learning.

  ● Use different noises to gain the class's attention: a bell, a buzzer, a short burst of music, a percussive instrument.

  ● Use music with a sense of urgency to give a short time frame for a task (for example, the theme from 'Mission Impossible').

  ● Add interest to your voice by talking in a different accent, using a range of tones or whispering.

  ● Teach mnemonics to aid memory in science or history.

  ● Get the children to warm up their voices and their brains by saying tongue twisters.

  ● When asking questions, get everyone to shout out their answers together.

● Here are some ways of adding a visual element to your lessons.

  ● Give the children coloured cards to indicate their grasp of a subject: green for *I'm fine and understand well*, orange for *I'm okay but not 100 per cent sure*, and red for *I need help*.

  ● Do collage activities with the class; give the children a pile of magazines and ask them to cut out different photos to make up a picture.

  ● Whenever you have to talk to the class to explain something, think about adding pictures, symbols, photographs, short video clips and so on to aid their understanding.

● Here are some ideas for practical ways of including movement-based activities.

  ● Use short exercises to break up longer periods of learning; for example, patting heads with one hand and rubbing circles on stomachs with the other.

  ● Find physical ways of demonstrating concepts; for example, showing division by dividing up the pupils into same-sized groups.

  ● To move the class from one place to another, add a dramatic intent; for example, with heavy feet, across a bed of nails, in slow motion.

You Can... **Use thinking displays**

Displays can be very static; a way of presenting and celebrating our children's completed work. However, displays can also be used to encourage and develop thinking and as an integral part of lessons.

Thinking points

● It is great if displays look good, but if their aim is to enhance learning, then this should not be the main focus.

● Displays that encourage thinking could look quite messy. They will be in a process of constant change, as children add ideas, thoughts, messages and so on.

● Think about when to include displays in the learning process. Sometimes they might act as a precursor to a topic, for example giving the children background information.

● At other times they might mirror class work as it progresses, with items being added at the end of each lesson.

Tips, ideas and activities

● Create a sense of 'interactivity' in your displays. See them as living, moving pieces of learning, rather than a 'snapshot' of finished work. You could:
  ○ Incorporate a range of media, for example a laptop playing a PowerPoint presentation or a CD player and headphones for listening activities.
  ○ Have a strong sensory element, for example including tactile objects or 'scratch and sniff' pads.
  ○ Create a 'starter' display to which you add as a topic unfolds.
  ○ Ask questions within a display, encouraging pupils to add their answers.
  ○ Use sticky notes for pupils to add their thoughts to any display.
  ○ Create lift-up flaps to encourage interest and interaction.
  ○ Have a competition to find a 'hidden' symbol within one of your displays.
  ○ Use Velcro so that pictures, words and so on can be moved around.
  ○ Add tables with objects to be handled and explored.
  ○ Find ways of adding a three-dimensional aspect to your displays.
  ○ Look at different spaces and places for displays: the ceiling, floors and windows, as well as the walls.

● Have one display that changes weekly, to get your children into the habit of interacting with display work. Put your weekly display in a prominent position, where the children can easily look at, refer to and interact with it. You might choose a 'theme of the week' for this display, for example:
  ○ 'Word of the week'; a key word from that week's lessons, or one that the children have difficulty spelling.
  ○ 'Thought of the week'; a 'big idea' for the children to explore.
  ○ 'Quote of the week'; a quote to inspire thinking (see the website www.wisdomquotes.com for ideas).
  ○ 'Topic of the week'; a range of information related to work in lessons or to a forthcoming trip.
  ○ 'Pupil of the week'; one child brings in photos and objects from home to tell the class about themselves.

You Can... Encourage thinking in your staff

If your staff feel that they all play a key part in making decisions about what happens at their school, this will inevitably help them feel more involved and engaged with their work. Look at ways of getting all staff, not just teachers, to think and work together.

Thinking points
● The nature of the job means that primary teachers can become isolated in their classrooms. Finding ways to break this isolation will aid innovation and good practice.

● Although continuity and consistency are very helpful in a school, it is also important for fresh ideas and approaches to be used.

● Keeping up-to-date with all the latest ideas about teaching can prove very time consuming. Getting staff to share their thinking and to talk together about what they have tried, will help them find the best new methods to use.

Tips, ideas and activities
● Find ways for your staff to share good ideas and good practice. This could involve:
  ● Using meeting time to think about innovative ways of improving the school, as well as for the more routine things you cover.
  ● Allowing staff to swap classes, so that they get a chance to see different age groups at work and try out new approaches.
  ● Giving newer teachers the opportunity to watch their more experienced colleagues at work on a regular basis.
  ● Rotating teaching assistants and learning support assistants around the year groups, so that they get to see different children and different teaching styles.
  ● Experimenting with new ways of timetabling. For example, you might try out some vertical groupings or get teachers to work with their subject specialism across different year groups.
  ● Bringing in some team teaching sessions, where two classes are put together in a large space to be taught by two or more staff at once.
  ● Doing some 'demonstration lessons' in staff training time. Ask for a group of pupil volunteers to be a mock class, to show how an unusual lesson activity works.
● Encourage staff to think about how they manage pupil behaviour and learning and what they can learn from other people's approaches. To achieve this, you could have an 'ideas board' in the staff room, where people can post:
  ● tips about strategies that have worked well
  ● positive comments about a child who has changed his or her behaviour
  ● non-confidential information that staff might like to know and comment on, for example that a child has been picked to star in the school play
  ● useful website addresses, for example to find information on dyslexia (www.dyslexia-inst.org.uk).
  ● ideas about good resources, new books or innovative teaching methods.

You Can... Create a healthy school

The better the environment around us, the more we tend to be able to focus and learn within that place. Get your children thinking about how to create a healthier school environment.

Thinking points

● Good eating habits and plenty of water, can really aid concentration. Encourage your children to bring water bottles into the classroom. Good hydration will really help with the development of thinking skills.

● A healthy lifestyle can also help children with their behaviour. You might have noticed that children who have a lot of sugary drinks tend to be more hyperactive in your lessons.

● Don't forget your own entitlement to a healthy workplace; if your room is not 'healthy' for the children, it will not be helping you work to your best as a teacher either.

Tips, ideas and activities

● Ask your children to think of ways to make the whole school environment healthier. Get them to think of ideas under a number of headings, for example:
  ○ healthy eating and drinking
  ○ healthy environments (classrooms, offices, playground)
  ○ recycling
  ○ exercise
  ○ managing stress
  ○ health and safety.

● Set up teams across the school, giving each team responsibility for analysing and improving one aspect of the overall health of the organisation.

● Take your class around the school to audit and assess potential danger areas. Study health and safety legislation (look at www.hse.gov.uk) to see where your school might be below recommended standards.

● Explore how the temperature of our environment can affect the way that we work. Take temperature readings in your classroom and ask the pupils to analyse their mood when it is too hot or too cold.

● Create a series of weekly themes in your canteen, to encourage the children to experiment with different healthy foods and tastes. Link some bright, interesting and tactile displays to each theme. For example:
  ○ Foods from around the world week
  ○ Fruit/vegetable week
  ○ Vegetarian week
  ○ Ditch the junk food week.

● Look at ways of managing stress and increasing a sense of relaxation in both staff and pupils. You could:
  ○ teach self-massage techniques to the pupils
  ○ arrange for teachers to have a head massage at lunchtimes
  ○ organise some meditation sessions
  ○ ask staff to try having one 'work free' evening a week.

● Ask your children to think about healthy attitudes towards each other and how they can build a more respectful school environment. This could mean:
  ○ remembering to be polite, having a 'please and thank you' day
  ○ taking care of younger school mates
  ○ treating everyone with respect, teachers, staff, friends, class mates.

You Can... Think about improving your playground

The development of thinking is not confined to the classroom. Your children exercise their minds, as well as their bodies, when they are outdoors. Making the most of your playground space will help you develop thinking across your school.

Thinking points

● With a crowded curriculum, children have more need than ever of the freedom offered by a playground.

● Being outdoors gives your pupils a chance to let off steam between lessons. It also allows them to develop imagination and creativity through unstructured play.

● We sometimes overlook the numerous opportunities for using outdoor spaces during lessons. A playground offers a place to make a mess with sand or water; it also provides a useful location for many science activities.

● When you take your class outside to work, lay down clear boundaries first. Finding themselves in an open space might be an overwhelming temptation for some of your more challenging pupils!

Tips, ideas and activities

● Base some topic work around your playground, looking at how it could be improved. This will work best if the school makes at least some of the changes that the children propose. Here are some ideas:

○ Conduct an audit of your outdoor space. Ask the children to gather information by making sketches, taking photos, taking measurements and so on.

○ Find out how the space is currently used and put this information into a database. Look at usage by children of different genders and different ages, examining any potential bias.

○ Ask the class to conduct research to help them consider the changes they might make. They could interview other pupils, talk to staff, study health and safety legislation and so on.

○ Encourage the pupils to think about playground use during lesson time, as well as at break time. For example, incorporating a natural area for science work, or painting grids on the floor to use in maths lessons.

○ Consider more unusual ideas: remodelling the landscape, creating a sculpture walk or setting up a city farm.

○ Think in different dimensions; look at the potential for using 'up' (for example, climbing frames) and 'down' (for example, a sunken seating area).

○ Ask the children to create a design for a new playground, individually, in groups, or as a whole class. Devise a competition to find the best design, perhaps judged by the other pupils at the school.

○ Ask your class to think about funding the project, working out how much it will cost and how to raise the money.

○ Encourage them to think laterally about finances. For example, a local garden centre might be willing to provide some plants; a play equipment company could donate some climbing frames.

○ Get the whole school involved in the project; for example, holding a school fair to raise funds, or getting other classes to help dig out a new garden area.

You Can... **Develop thinking as a school community**

Where the school works together as a whole, this has a powerful effect on the learning that takes place. Find ways to develop thinking right across your school, making the children feel part of a community.

Thinking points

● A positive (or negative) ethos is something that can only be built by the school community as a whole. When the ethos is a positive one, this permeates right through the school and makes life easier and happier for everyone.

● Where the children feel a sense of responsibility for their schoolmates, this will help to create positive attitudes both inside and outside of the classroom.

● Positive peer pressure from children at the top end of the school can have a very beneficial impact on behaviour and learning throughout the organisation.

Tips, ideas and activities

● Have a 'thinking time' each week when the whole school does the same thinking activity, across all year groups. You might ask pupils to keep a scrapbook of thoughts and thinking. You could have a different theme each week in 'thinking time', for example, logic, philosophy, creativity and so on.

● Create a 'thinking' display area in a prominent area of the school. Use this for pupils to share examples of the thinking going on in their classrooms. Give the children responsibility for the area, setting up a rota so that the display changes every couple of weeks or so.

● Consider holding a 'collapse' day, when the normal timetable is put aside and the pupils work together on a single topic. On a 'collapse' day, the staff organise a range of different activities around a central theme. For example, on a themed day about 'The Victorians', there might be:

- demonstrations of Victorian-style cookery in the canteen
- a mock-up of a Victorian classroom, with teachers using 'old fashioned' discipline methods
- examples of Victorian clothing
- Victorian games in the playground.

● Teaching is a great way to extend our own learning and to develop empathy for others. Arrange for the older children to go into their younger counterparts' classrooms on occasions, to help with lessons. The pupils could:

- help individuals with their reading
- sit and work with groups during a lesson to give additional help
- read a story to the class
- give an oral presentation that they have researched and prepared in your lessons.

● Find lots of ways to give the children ownership of what goes on in their school: school councils, ideas boxes, buddy schemes and so on.

● Organise some projects where the whole school works together to improve the learning environment. For example:

- a recycling project
- creating a new nature area in the playground
- renovating an old classroom.

You Can... Think about the primary–secondary transfer

Research has shown that children will often drop back in their academic performance as they move up to secondary school. Thinking with your pupils about the transfer will help them cope better with the changes involved.

Thinking points

● There is a limit to what individual teachers can do to ease the transfer. Much of the success of the transfer lies with the primary and secondary school as a whole.

● We tend to be fearful of the unknown and will often blow our fears out of proportion to the reality of a situation.

● Giving your children a better understanding of what the transfer involves will help them feel more in control.

● Children face many changes in the transfer, not least adapting from having one teacher to having many. They can also find it difficult to move around the school for lessons, rather than having a single classroom base.

Tips, ideas and activities

● Work as a school to ease the transfer for your pupils. For example, you could organise:
  ● Visits to secondary schools during term time, to see lessons in progress and meet new teachers.
  ● Meetings between Year 6 and Year 7 staff, to discuss curriculum continuity and children with special needs.
  ● Cross-phase schemes of work to be started in Year 6 and completed in Year 7.
  ● Older children at the secondary schools to act as 'buddies' and help the new pupils settle in.

● Talk with your children about their feelings as the end of Year 6 approaches. Ask them to think about their worries, what these are and how they might be overcome. For example they might be concerned about:
  ● mixing with older pupils
  ● getting lost on a large school site
  ● bullying
  ● academic pressure
  ● quantities of homework
  ● losing old friends and making new ones.

● Your children will also feel excited about going up to the 'big school'. Ask them to think about the positive sides of the move, for example:
  ● meeting older pupils
  ● following an older sibling already at secondary school
  ● having access to a range of specialist facilities and equipment
  ● trying out new topics and learning new subjects.

● Help your children to devise lots of practical coping tactics and strategies. For example:
  ● Get well organised: packing their bags the night before school, laying out uniform ready to get dressed, buying a folder or using a school diary to keep all their important papers together.
  ● Speak up; encourage them to ask for help if they need it, approaching a form tutor if they have any questions or concerns.
  ● Locate the key places; advise your pupils to mark the most important places on a map of the school, for example their form room, the toilets, the dining hall.

You Can... Use the seasons to inspire thinking

The seasons give a shape to the year and help us to see the passing of time. Thinking about seasonal changes in the environment offers many opportunities for scientific exploration. It can also inspire some interesting creative and imaginative work.

Thinking points

- Looking at the local environment in the different seasons will encourage your children to think about the natural world around them.

- In a city, there might be less obvious signs of change. Taking your class to an outdoor space will help the children develop their thinking about the environment.

- Tracking changes over the course of a year helps your children become more aware of the passing of time and of the cycles of natural life.

- Various festivals fall during each season, marking out the passing of the year. Explore how the symbolism of festivals often links to what is happening in nature (for example, the symbol of light used in winter festivals).

Tips, ideas and activities

- Think about how the seasons affect a view. Take your class to a local park or other outdoor space. Ask the children to choose a view that will change over the year (for example, one with deciduous trees). Ask the class to:
  - make a sketch, drawing or painting
  - take a photograph or video footage
  - collect natural 'found objects' for a collage or sculpture
  - think of words inspired by the view for a poem
  - sketch some shapes to use in a dance.

- Return to the same location over the year, once in each season. In the summer term, create finished artwork based on the seasonal changes. Ask the children to share their work with the class, talking about the thinking behind it. Create a display and invite other children or parents to a viewing.

- Explore how plants change with the seasons. Bring in examples of plants with particularly interesting seasonal features. You could ask your local garden centre to lend you some plants for demonstrations, or approach a keen gardener at school for samples. For example:
  - Spring – bulbs. Examine the bulb's storage system; cut one open to see what's inside. Ask the children to think about how the bulb gathers food and nutrients for the following year through its leaves.
  - Summer – annual flowers. Look at pollinating insects and how cross-fertilisation within a species produces new flower colours. (Sweet peas are particularly good for exploring this.)
  - Autumn – trees with autumn colour (such as maple). Explore the range of bright leaf colours and think about why leaves change colour. See the website www.best gardening.com/bgc/howto/botany04.htm for a useful explanation. The Royal Forestry Society website (www.rfs.org.uk/) also has lots of helpful information.
  - Winter – plants with strongly scented flowers (such as, Christmas Box or *Sarcococca*). Think about why plants that flower at this time tend to be strongly scented (to attract the few pollinating insects around in the winter).

You Can... Think about the symbolism of Christmas

We are surrounded by symbols: letters, words, numbers, road signs, musical notes and computer icons. All of these things and many more are symbolic representations; they 'stand for' something else. Christmas is a time that has many symbols, both religious and mythical.

Thinking points

● Often children see only what is obvious and apparent; they are unaware of how a picture, a piece of writing, a sculpture, might have further layers of significance hidden within it.

● The ability to think about and understand how symbols and metaphors work is a higher-order thinking skill. It allows your children access to these deeper levels of meaning.

● Festivals are often full of symbolic associations, many of which have a long historical precedent.

● Exploring how these symbols work will give your children a fuller insight into the meanings and traditions of the Christmas celebrations. It will hopefully encourage them to extend their thinking beyond the shallow, commercialised side of the festivities.

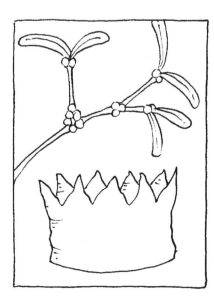

Tips, ideas and activities

● Introduce the concept of symbols; show your children some images and ask them to talk about what these 'mean' and how they gain meaning from them. For example, road signs, colours, trademarks (Nike, McDonalds and so on).

● Ask your class to create a mind map of the things that they associate with Christmas. Look through their suggestions, searching for those that are potentially symbolic.

● Talk about how symbols can have a number of associations. For example, candles symbolise Jesus as the light of the world, but are also linked to ancient ideas about the rebirth of the sun at the winter solstice.

● Explore the historical roots of different Christmas traditions. Divide your children into groups to do some thinking on the subject. Give each group a different object that has symbolical associations with this time of year. Ask them to create a spidergram of all the words and ideas that their symbolic item might contain. For example:

  ● a candle
  ● a wrapped present
  ● a Christmas card
  ● a sprig of holly or ivy
  ● a branch of mistletoe
  ● a paper crown from a cracker.

● Rotate the items around the groups, gathering the thinking of the class. Create large mind maps for a display that brings together all their ideas.

● Look at the website www.whychristmas.com for some useful explanations of many Christmas customs and traditions.

● Set your children a 'thinking task' for the Christmas holidays. When they take their Christmas cards down, ask them to keep any that they think use symbolic images. Look through these in January and talk about how the symbolism works in each one.

● Explore the roots and symbolism of some other traditional British celebrations. Look at the festivals section on the website www.mysteriousbritain.co.uk/. This gives the background to a range of folk festivals throughout the year.

You Can... Use holidays as a theme for thinking

For both teachers and children, the school holidays offer a chance to rest, relax and recuperate. For those of us lucky enough to go away somewhere new, a holiday can also offer a valuable learning experience.

Thinking points

● Holidays offer a way of dividing up the passing of time; they give a pattern to the course of the school year.

● There are often changes in the school routine in the run-up to a holiday period. This might mean the children start pushing the boundaries of learning and behaviour.

● Going on holiday allows us to sample new countries and cultures, and increase our historical and geographical understanding.

● When using this theme, be sensitive to the fact that some of your pupils might not go away anywhere during the school breaks.

Tips, ideas and activities

● Ask your class to think about where the word 'holiday' comes from, by looking at the word itself. Do some research into the roots of the word. Talk about what the word 'holiday' means to us today and how its original meanings have changed.
● Talk with your children about which holidays they particularly like. This might be specific times of year (Christmas, summer) or different types of holiday (adventure, overseas travel).
● Create some postcards home from exotic destinations, the more unusual the better! Encourage the children to think laterally, for example sending postcards home from an alien planet.
● Create an imaginative activity based on packing for a holiday.
  ● Enter the room as a character; someone who has terrible trouble deciding what to pack when they go on holiday.
  ● Bring in with you a small suitcase and a huge pile of clothes and other items that you want to take with you.
  ● Tell the class the destination of your holiday, either hot (such as Africa) or cold (such as, Greenland).
  ● Ask the pupils to think about which clothes and other items you need to take with you, and how you can fit the maximum amount in your case.
  ● Give the class a maximum weight limit for the suitcase.
● Use the holiday topic for some mathematical thinking with an environmental theme. For example:
  ● Create a mind map of all the different ways of travelling to go on holiday.
  ● Discuss the environmental impact of these methods of travel.
  ● Use a map to check the distances to popular holiday destinations, home and abroad.
  ● Measure the CO_2 emissions of flying to each of these destinations. Use the website www.climatecare.org and click on 'CO_2 calculators'.
● Create a 'countdown' to holiday periods in your classroom, for example by using a calendar from ten days to zero. This will help keep the class focused on work and encourage a positive sense of anticipation.

You Can... Think about approaching exams

Formal tests are not necessarily a good way of testing or developing thinking skills. However, they are a fact of school life which starts at primary level and continues on into higher education.

Thinking points

● To an extent, success in exams is about being willing to 'play the game'. Whatever your personal opinion about formalised testing, you need to help your children understand the strategies for doing well in exams.

● As adults we will have developed our own strategies for taking and passing exams. Don't assume that your pupils will know this; help them think about good exam technique rather than letting them learn from their mistakes.

● Some children will cope well with the pressure of exams, whilst others will find it almost impossible to stay calm. Take emotional needs into account as well as focusing on learning and skills.

Tips, ideas and activities

● Talk through previous exam papers with your class, familiarising the children with the layout and type of questions. You could ask:
  ● What is this question asking you?
  ● What does the examiner want to see in your answer?
  ● How many marks are available?
  ● How much should you write to earn those marks?
  ● How long should you spend on this question?

● Think about timing with your class; this is a classic area where children fall down. Discuss with your pupils how:
  ● Time should be spent first on reading through questions/ texts/the paper.
  ● Where appropriate, time spent on planning will lead to a better answer.
  ● Time spent should relate to the number of marks available.
  ● If they get stuck, they should move on to the next question.

● Encourage your children to use spidergrams for both revision and planning during an exam. As a structure, a diagram offers a great way of making brief and easily-accessible notes. For longer exam answers, pupils should create a single diagram for each paragraph, with about four points within it. This helps them remember to paragraph and also to include the appropriate number of ideas.

● Help your children find strategies to handle their nerves:
  ● Spending plenty of time on revision and practice.
  ● Eating, drinking and sleeping well.
  ● Pausing and breathing deeply at the beginning of an exam.
  ● Remembering that exam success is not the 'be-all and end-all'!

● Do some visualisation exercises with the children, to help them relax and feel more confident.
  ● Get your pupils sitting or lying in a relaxed position.
  ● Ask them to close their eyes.
  ● Talk them through a calming and relaxing scenario (for example, sitting on a warm, sunny beach).
  ● Once fully relaxed, talk them through a positive visualisation of taking an exam.

You Can... **Explore how time affects behaviour**

Our behaviour can change in dramatic ways in the run up to, or the aftermath of, important times and events in our lives. Thinking about how we are affected by time, place and situation gives us insight into our psychological processes.

Thinking points

● Time plays an important role in schools because it helps us to create routines. However, the structures we create will not necessarily tie in with our children's body clocks.

● Sometimes we have to force our pupils to work at times when they are not in the right frame of mind. This can lead to frustrated children and teachers, and to poor standards of work.

● You might have found particular difficulties with concentration and behaviour on Friday afternoons and in the dark winter months. If possible, it is a good idea to take this into account by adapting your teaching.

● Exploring the effects of time on their behaviour will help your children understand why they feel tired or irritated at certain times of the week. Hopefully, it will also help them better control their moods.

Tips, ideas and activities

● Ask your children to think about their emotional state at different times of the day, week or year. Discuss why long, sunny summer days can make them happy, whilst short, dark winter days might make them feel down.

● As a class, keep a log of the children's moods from Monday to Friday. This will give you an insight into the best times for particular activities.

● The time of day or year in relation to events can have a dramatic effect on human thought processes. Use the drama exercise below to explore this concept further.

  ● Use a large open space, such as the hall or gym.
  ● Split the class into groups of between four and six pupils.
  ● Create an area for each group by using four chairs to mark squares.

● Give the children a situation with a time factor. Here are some suggestions:

  ● thirty seconds before friends arrive for your birthday party
  ● five minutes before the first day of school
  ● five minutes before the end of term
  ● one minute before sitting an exam
  ● ten seconds after taking an exam which went badly
  ● thirty seconds before playing in the FA Cup final
  ● one minute after losing the FA Cup final
  ● twenty seconds before a comet hits the Earth

● The children have a few moments to discuss the scenario before you say 'Go'.

  ● They then start an improvisation. After a few minutes, say 'Freeze'.
  ● Now:

  a) ask the children to think about how this situation/time affected their behaviour or
  b) get groups to show their improvisations or
  c) move onto the next scenario.

● Experiment with quantities of time, exploring the difference between 'twenty seconds' and 'five minutes'.

● Start with familiar events then move on to situations where they have to use more imagination.

You Can... **Build a sense of team work**

Sometimes a class will 'gel' naturally and work well together as a whole unit. On other occasions, there will be tension between different groups within the class. Where this happens, children will need to think more about their relationships in order to avoid difficulties arising with both learning and behaviour.

Thinking points

● Getting children to work well together is not necessarily easy. Even as adults, we can find it difficult to accommodate the ideas and foibles of our peers.

● Where the majority of children in a class feel a sense of team work, there will be a positive influence on any minority who wish to disrupt the learning. Peer pressure is a very powerful tool for changing behaviour.

● Many of the exercises that develop thinking skills will need the children to work in groups, whether as a whole class or in a small group situation.

● When group work is done well and with a cooperative attitude, the learning of all your pupils will be enhanced.

Tips, ideas and activities

● From the start, insist that your pupils work with everyone. Get them used to working in boy/girl pairs and they won't think to question it. Similarly, don't allow them to pick partners based on social preference; insist that they are willing to work in random groups.

● Be careful when using competitive strategies to encourage hard work. Done sparingly, encouraging the children to compete can help create a sense of focus and commitment. However, if over-used it can lead to a desire to 'win whatever it takes'.

● Try a drama exercise called 'Win the Chair' to encourage the children to work together and to develop quick thinking. In this activity, the idea of 'beating the teacher' adds elements of competition and humour, but against you rather than each other.

  ● Stand the children in a circle and put one chair in the middle.
  ● Explain that the object of the exercise is for the pupils to stop you from sitting down on the chair and consequently 'winning' it.
  ● They do this by keeping the chair in constant use.
  ● They can 'use' it in any way they wish (within reason), by coming into the centre and involving it in a short performance.
    ● For example, the chair might be a car seat, an aeroplane seat, a throne, a hiding place, a cooker, an animal and so on.
    ● It is up to the class to decide whose 'turn' it is to use the seat. Do not advise them on this.
    ● At first, you will probably find it easy to 'win' the chair, as the children dither about coming into the middle.
    ● Eventually, the pupils will realise that they need to either:
    a) be quick to run into the centre if no one else does or
    b) decide on a method for taking turns as a team (such as going round the circle).

You Can... **Think about community**

Where people have a sense of community, this helps create a feeling of belonging and security. 'Community' means different things to different people. For some, it is about belonging to a particular area; for others it is about belonging to a faith group.

Thinking points

● There is, perhaps, less feeling of community in our busy, modern world. Children living in a city environment might feel cut off from the people in their local area, perhaps because of a lack of community facilities.

● Similarly, although rural communities can offer a strong sense of community, some children might not feel as though they 'belong'.

● If we feel part of a place or a people, we are far more likely to take care of our environment and look out for our fellow human beings.

● The school also offers a type of community; one that is inclusive of all peoples, regardless of culture, faith, ability, wealth and so on.

Tips, ideas and activities

● Encourage some general thinking about the concept of 'community'. Ask:
  ◉ What is a 'community'?
  ◉ What different sorts of community are there?
  ◉ Who is in your community?
  ◉ What helps create a sense of community?
  ◉ Do you have a strong sense of community? Who or what creates this?
  ◉ Is community about a geographical area?
  ◉ Is community about having similar beliefs or values?
  ◉ How can a sense of community be increased?
  ◉ Does a community have a duty of care to those within it who need extra help?
  ◉ What should happen to those who damage or are disrespectful within a community?

● Use the following quote from Winston Churchill to inspire thinking: 'There is no finer investment for any community than putting milk into babies.' Encourage your pupils to see the layers of meaning in what Churchill said, to look beyond the literal meaning of 'milk' and consider what else he might have meant.

● Create a three-dimensional model of a community in some design and technology sessions. Ask the class to:
  ◉ Choose a location for the community (such as, city, small town, village, in this country or overseas).
  ◉ Decide what to put into the community (such as, shops, mosque, school, park, library, GP's surgery, as well as houses).
  ◉ Sketch a design to plan the layout of the area.
  ◉ Choose some modelling materials, (such as, junk modelling, Lego, clay).
  ◉ Work in teams to model different parts of the community.

● Once the model is finished, throw some problems at the community and ask the children to think about how the community should respond. For example:
  ◉ The council wants to house a 'problem family' nearby.
  ◉ There is a fire which destroys several houses.
  ◉ A large supermarket chain wants to open a new shop in the area.

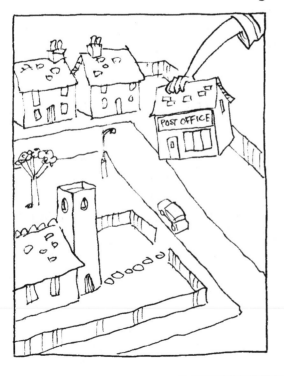

You Can... Develop understanding of a range of viewpoints

Some topics raise strong emotions and divergent opinions. Being able to understand and respect how others think, despite our differences, is a key step on the path to empathy.

Thinking points

● We might not agree with what others believe, but we can still respect their right to hold a different opinion.

● Sometimes, a strong opinion can tip over into prejudice and even incitement to hatred. Maintaining our freedom of speech, whilst protecting people as necessary, can be a tricky balancing act.

● Children and young people will often hold very strong, clear and passionate views on contentious topics.

● Understanding the subtleties of an issue might only come with age and experience. As we grow older, we see that there are often areas of grey within an apparently black or white argument.

Tips, ideas and activities

● Use a council meeting format to explore a range of viewpoints.
   ● Arrange the classroom with a line of chairs at the front for the characters 'running' the meeting and the rest of the chairs in rows, facing front.
   ● Choose confident volunteers to play the people leading the meeting.
   ● The rest of the children play a character of their own choice.
● Try different scenarios, choosing ideas that elicit strong opinions, for example:
   ● Selling off the local library building to a supermarket. The pupils could play councillors, the supermarket manager, local people looking for jobs, parents and children, teachers and so on.
   ● Allowing a mobile phone mast to be erected in the school playground.
● Talk about the quote: 'I disapprove of what you say, but I will fight to the death for your right to say it'. Ask:
   ● What does the quote mean?
   ● Why would we support someone's right to an opinion, even though we disagree with it?
   ● How would it feel if you were not allowed to express your viewpoint?
   ● Are there some things that people should not have the right to say?
● Bring in a range of head gear: a police hat, teacher's mortarboard, builder's hat, old lady's hat, nurse's hat and so on. Invite volunteers to wear the hats and become that person. Quiz them (in character) about their views on different subjects: hunting, graffiti, animal testing and so on.
● Hold a class debate with a twist.
   ● Choose a topic to debate, for example, 'Testing on animals should be made illegal'.
   ● Ask the children to split themselves into two sides; for and against the motion.
   ● Encourage the pupils to list the key points they wish to make during the debate, writing these in brief on cards.
   ● Ask the two sides to swap their cards. Hold the debate, with the children arguing the opposite view to the one they actually believe.

You Can... Develop a sense of personal responsibility

As they grow older, children need to start taking more responsibility for the way that they treat themselves and others. Our ability to develop a conscience is a key part of what makes us human.

Thinking points

● We live in a society where our behaviour towards others is closely regulated. Rather than developing a sense of personal responsibility, we are often told what we can and cannot do by the state.

● Feeling a sense of responsibility for ourselves and for the welfare of others, is vital to creating a moral code. For some, this will be part of a religious way of life; for others it will be based on what the individual conscience dictates.

● It can be hard for individuals to speak out against what they see as wrong. This might be on a large scale, for example standing up to an oppressive state; it might also be on a small scale, for example sticking up for a child who is being bullied.

Tips, ideas and activities

● Develop thinking around the subject of personal responsibility, using this extract from an anti-Nazi speech by German pastor Martin Niemöller (see the website www.history.ucsb.edu/faculty/marcuse/niem.htm):

> First they came for the Jews
> and I did not speak out, because I was not a Jew.
> Then they came for the Communists
> and I did not speak out, because I was not a Communist.
> Then they came for the trade unionists
> and I did not speak out, because I was not a trade unionist.
> Then they came for me
> and by then there was no one left to speak out for me.

● You might talk about:
  ○ the historical background to the speech
  ○ why the pastor did not speak out
  ○ why the German people did not stand up against Hitler
  ○ whether some people have a greater personal responsibility than others.

● Create a whole-class dramatisation of this speech. Hold a class assembly on the theme of 'personal responsibility' and use this dramatisation to open up your presentation.

● Think about how far we are responsible for our own actions and how far others should take care of us. Talk about the recent court cases against fast food outlets, where people sued for compensation when they became overweight. You might like to show your class some extracts from the film *Super Size Me* by Morgan Spurlock to illustrate the discussion.

● Use this 'Flour babies' exercise, based on the book of the same name by Anne Fine, to look at the issue of personal responsibility.
  ○ Give the children a bag of flour each.
  ○ Explain that this is their 'baby' and that they must care for it for a week.
  ○ They must supervise their 'babies' at all times; if they go out in the evening they must organise a babysitter.
  ○ At the end of the week, talk with the children about how it felt to be responsible for someone else.

You Can... Explore rights and responsibilities

The young people of today are, thankfully, very much aware of their rights. However, alongside an awareness of their entitlements, it is also important for children to realise that they have responsibilities in return.

Thinking points

● Many people in the world are not given access to even the most basic human rights. Thinking about this will help your children appreciate what they have.

● Understanding that with rights come responsibilities forms the basis for good behaviour. Thinking on this issue can lead to improved attitudes from your children in the classroom and beyond.

● Building a sense of responsibility for others will help your pupils develop empathy and understanding. It will also help them work more cooperatively during group activities.

Tips, ideas and activities

● Conduct a mind map exercise with your pupils of all the things they 'want'. Now make a spidergram of all the things they actually 'need'. Talk about the differences between the two; which items on the list should be classed as their 'rights'?

● Create two collages; one for 'I want' and another for 'I need'.

● Ask the children to imagine that they are stranded on a desert island. In groups, invite them to talk about what they might need to survive. If they could only have three items, what would these be and why?

● Now ask the children to think about the things that are not essential for physical survival, but which we need for well-being. Their list might include love, friendship, companionship, trust and so on.

● Get your pupils to play some trust games, talking about the kind of responsibilities they owe to their classmates while playing these games. Here are some suggestions:

○ 'I'm falling'– The children stand in a circle, with one person in the middle. The person shouts 'I'm falling' and then falls, keeping their body rigid. The rest of the group must move to catch the person.

○ 'Obstacle course' – The children lead a blindfolded partner around a course made up of tables and chairs, using only instructions spoken quietly in the partner's ear.

○ 'The raft' – The children work in groups with a large piece of paper acting as the 'raft'. The children must balance as many people on their 'raft' as possible.

● Ask the class to research the rights that are granted to them by law. You could look at www.humanrights.gov.uk for more information.

● Consider getting a class pet; this helps children develop a great sense of responsibility. Create a rota so that all the pupils take a part in feeding, cleaning and so on. If a class pet sounds too onerous, a few pot plants offer a cheaper and simpler alternative.

You Can... **Create a climate for philosophical discussion**

Managing discussions of a philosophical nature requires skill and sensitivity from the teacher. Children can sometimes be quite intransigent in their views and attitudes; you will need to encourage them to think widely and freely.

Thinking points

● Taking part in philosophical discussions can give your children a strong sense of personal empowerment. They get to explore and develop their own views on a range of concepts, including some tricky ones.

● For those pupils brought up in a household where strong views are held, it might prove difficult to question these ideas and opinions.

● Clear boundaries and limits need to be set in order to make philosophical discussion work.

● Making philosophical discussion a key part of classroom activity will help your children develop their higher-order thinking skills.

Tips, ideas and activities

● Talk with your class about what they think 'philosophy' means, and the type of subjects that might be covered during a philosophical discussion.

● Explore where the word 'philosophy' comes from. Look at the website http://krysstal.com/borrow_greek.html to see the huge range of words that the English language borrows from Greek.

● Discuss, consider and agree some clear ground rules for philosophical discussions with your class. Look at the appropriate attitudes that pupils should demonstrate. For example:
  ● be willing to participate and to ask questions
  ● listen carefully to what others have to say
  ● think carefully before they speak
  ● respect other people's opinions and views.

● Think about the aims of philosophical discussions; for example to learn to:
  ● express ideas clearly and concisely
  ● stay open to new ideas
  ● be willing to reconsider opinions
  ● use a range of thinking skills
  ● take time to reflect on what has been discussed afterwards.

● Make it clear to your pupils that your discussions are not about giving 'right' or 'wrong' answers. Spend time talking about how people will have and are entitled to have, their own ideas and opinions on different subjects.

● Here is one possible format for philosophical sessions:
  ● Show the class a stimulus to get them thinking, for example: a story that raises philosophical questions, an image, a prop, a poem and so on.
  ● Work with the class to gather a list of questions to discuss.
  ● Decide on one interesting idea to use for an extended discussion.

● You could look at the website www.philosophyforkids.com for some more ideas on using philosophy with children.

You Can... **Think about morality**

For children, issues of morality are often viewed in the simplest terms of right or wrong. Exploring the complexity of some moral issues is a good way to develop and extend their thinking.

Thinking points

● For children brought up within a strongly religious framework, ideas of 'right' or 'wrong' will often be dictated by the moral code of their faith.

● Children might find it difficult to question their thinking on this subject. You will need to be sensitive to different beliefs when posing questions to the class.

● Thinking about what 'good' and 'bad' mean will help your children to think about their behaviour. Seeing the impact that good or bad acts can have on others should help them to develop more empathetic attitudes.

Tips, ideas and activities

● Use a circle-time session to do some talking and thinking about issues of morality. Here are some starter questions to get your discussion going:
   ● What is 'good'?
   ● What is 'bad'?
   ● What is 'right'?
   ● What is 'wrong'?
   ● What is evil?
   ● Are people born evil, or is it a result of their upbringing?
   ● Can we ever do bad things to achieve a good end?
   ● Can we be good without believing in a god?

● Talk about atheism with the class. Ask the children to think about where morality comes from, if it is not based on a religious code. Use this quote from Abraham Lincoln to develop their thinking; 'When I do good, I feel good. When I do bad, I feel bad. That's my religion.'

● Pose some tricky moral dilemmas for your children, to get them thinking about shades of right and wrong. Here are some scenarios:
   ● You see a well-off pupil drop a £5 note in the playground. You need the money to buy a birthday present for your mother. What do you do?
   ● You give up sweets for Lent and get sponsorship. You are going to donate the money to charity. On the last day of Lent, a friend offers you a sweet and you eat it without thinking. Do you confess to your sponsors, even though they might not give you the money?
   ● A friend invites you to her birthday party, but tells you she is not going to invite another girl from your group because she no longer likes her. On the day of the party, the girl who has not been invited asks you to go to the cinema with her. What do you do?
   ● You are given the chance to go back in time and shoot Adolf Hitler. This would potentially save the lives of millions of people. Can it ever be right to commit murder?

You Can... Explore actions and consequences

The idea that actions have consequences is an important concept for children to grasp. It helps them to develop responsibility for their own behaviour, a key factor in successful learning.

Thinking points

● As far as it is sensible or safe, it is best for children to discover the natural consequences of their actions. Where young people learn by making their own mistakes, this motivates them not to repeat an action in the future.

● Sometimes, adults will need to apply external consequences to change a child's behaviour, for example removing privileges or applying sanctions. The younger the child, the more immediate the consequences must be, so that they make the link between the action and the outcome.

● The ideal is, of course, for children to learn to take responsibility for their actions without any external controls. In the wider world, society enforces consequences (such as, prison) on those who cannot stick to our laws and moral codes.

● The consequences of our actions can, of course, be positive as well as negative!

Tips, ideas and activities

● Use the photocopiable sheet on page 58 ('Chain of consequences'). This is designed to get your pupils looking at the chain of events that might be set in motion by a single action. The chains might include both positive and negative consequences. Before tackling the activity:
  ○ Talk through the concept of consequences with your class, thinking about how one action can lead on to others.
  ○ Discuss the concept of logic. Use the sheet to try out some sample chains of consequences that would make sense.
  ○ Ask the children to complete the sheet.

● A series of consequences offers a good way of creating a story outline. After completing their chains, ask your pupils to use them as the basis for a story.

● Discuss the religious belief that the way we behave in life will have consequences for us after we die. Explore the thinking of different faiths on this subject, for example, the concepts of:
  ○ heaven and hell
  ○ reincarnation
  ○ karma.

● Talk with your class about short- and long-term consequences, encouraging them to think beyond the immediate action–consequence. Give them some scenarios and ask them to consider the likely outcomes within different time scales. For example, a child who regularly misses school could:
  ○ Short term: find it hard to make friends and keep up with the learning
  ○ Medium term: fail exams or be suspended from school
  ○ Long term: be unable to get a job, get involved in crime to make money and end up in jail.

● Use Newton's third law of motion to encourage some thinking about consequences; 'For every action there is an opposite and equal reaction'. You could talk about:
  ○ the science behind this law
  ○ whether the law applies to human behaviour as well
  ○ whether we can 'get away with' bad actions without suffering consequences
  ○ whether a negative action can have positive consequences.

You Can... **Look at the way we treat animals**

The issue of our relationship with animals brings up lots of ethical questions. Young people can feel very strongly about this topic and will often take a very clear moral position.

Thinking points

● You might also have very strong personal views on what is 'right' and 'wrong' in the context of our relationship with animals. You will need to keep your personal position private during your discussions with the class.

● Although your children are perfectly entitled to hold strong, clear opinions, try to encourage them to see the issues from a range of different viewpoints. They do not have to change their minds about what they think, but they should be able to consider a subject from a variety of perspectives.

● With older pupils, you might like to address the idea of 'consciousness' and talk about whether any animals other than humans could be said to have a soul.

Tips, ideas and activities

● Talk about the different roles that animals play for humans and what ethical position your children take on using animals:
  - as pets
  - for clothing
  - for travel/work
  - for testing
  - for food
  - as companions/guides
  - for entertainment
  - for sport.

● Think about the different attitudes that people have to animals. Ask for volunteers to sit in a hot seat and stand up for the different viewpoints. For example:
  - a vegetarian
  - a vegan
  - an anti-vivisectionist/animal rights protestor
  - a cattle farmer
  - a fur hunter.

● Consider the use of animals for entertainment. Here are some questions for group or whole-class discussion:
  - What are your views on the use of animals in zoos and circuses?
  - If it is wrong to keep a tiger in a cage, is it also wrong to keep fish in an aquarium?
  - How do you feel about using animals for sports such as hunting, horse racing, greyhound racing, polo and shooting?
  - Do you think animals enjoy taking part in some sports?

● You might like to combine thinking on this subject with a visit to a local animal sanctuary, nature reserve or zoo.

● Here are some useful website addresses related to this topic:
  - www.rspca.org.uk – Royal Society for the Prevention of Cruelty to Animals
  - www.rspb.org.uk – Royal Society for the Protection of Birds
  - www.ufaw.org.uk – Universities Federation for Animal Welfare
  - www.fawc.org.uk – Farm Animal Welfare Council
  - www.nawt.org.uk – National Animal Welfare Trust
  - www.ciwf.org.uk – Compassion in World Farming
  - www.cawc.org.uk – Companion Animal Welfare Council
  - www.peta.org.uk – People for the Ethical Treatment of Animals
  - www.bornfree.org.uk – Born Free Foundation
  - www.medicalprogress.org – Coalition for Medical Progress

You Can... **Think about conserving resources**

Young people are often far more aware of environmental issues than adults are. Looking at the conservation of our planet's resources can encourage some interesting thinking about personal and collective responsibility.

Thinking points

● The issue of waste and recycling offers many interesting cross-curricular links, particularly with science.

● Thinking about this issue will help your children develop a sense of personal responsibility for their environment. It should encourage them to think on a more local scale as well, for example understanding why graffiti and vandalism are wrong.

● It can sometimes feel that environmental issues are far removed from the individual, that they are problems too big for one person to solve. Seeing how we can all make a difference will help your children feel a sense of self worth.

Tips, ideas and activities

● Create a mind map of the resources that we have on our planet. Ask your class to divide these into finite resources (such as oil and gas) and unlimited resources (such as wind and sun). Talk about why it is important to conserve the Earth's resources.
● Talk about the idea of personal responsibility for our environment.
  ● How much personal responsibility do we have for the planet?
  ● How much responsibility should government and businesses take?
  ● Can individuals make a difference?
  ● Can small changes to our lifestyles have an impact?
  ● What responsibilities do have for our immediate environment; our homes, our schools, our local area?
● Bring in a bin bag filled with rubbish. Include a mixture of items: some that can be reused, recycled or composted, others that cannot. For example:
  ● cardboard packaging
  ● plastic bottles
  ● tin foil
  ● tin cans
  ● fruit and vegetable peelings
  ● disposable nappies (unused, obviously!)
  ● batteries.
● Sort through the items, talking about what we can recycle and how this can be done. You could ask someone who works in your local council's recycling and waste department to talk to the class.
● Encourage your children to set up a school recycling scheme. Take the pupils around the school to do an audit of how waste is currently handled.
● Ask your pupils to maintain a 'rubbish log' at home over a weekend, itemising everything that goes in the bin.
● On a trip to the supermarket, ask the pupils to identify the top five 'best buys' environmentally and the top five 'worst offenders'. You could also look at the issue of 'food miles', identifying how far some fruit and vegetables have 'travelled' on a map.
● Create a compost heap in your school garden and teach the children about the science behind composting.

You Can... **Think about words**

A key feature of the human brain is its ability to decode words and find meaning in them. You can develop some really interesting thinking with your class by looking at words and how they work.

Thinking points

● Words offer a fascinating example of symbolism. They act as labels, with the object (a cat, a book) remaining the same, no matter what we call it.

● Different languages use a whole range of different alphabets and characters. There are also a variety of ways of presenting and reading text on a page.

● Etymology, or the study of the roots and origins of words, offers a fascinating insight into the history of a country. Understanding where words come from and how they are formed is also very useful for learning to spell.

● Babies are born with the ability to hear and speak the words of any language. By the age of around six months they have lost this facility and have started to hear only the language that their parents or carers speak.

Tips, ideas and activities

● Ask your class to think about their favourite words; what are they and why do they like them? Is it the sound or meaning that appeals? Invite volunteers to present a short summary of one favourite word to the class.

● Set a homework activity to bring in examples of familiar words in another language. (This is particularly effective if lots of pupils in the class are bi- or trilingual.) Create a display of one word written in a range of different languages and characters.

● Play a game of 'Dingbats'; this makes use of the double meanings of some words. The children draw a familiar word or phrase using pictures and symbols. The others must guess what the phrase is. For example, 'up to no good' could be '↑ 2 ~~good~~'. Play this game in groups, with the teacher providing the words and phrases. Alternatively, do it as a whole class activity, with volunteers coming to the front to draw.

● Explore palindromes (words spelt the same way both forwards and backwards). Look at some simple examples, such as *mum, nan, eye* and *noon*. Set a challenge for your children to hunt through the dictionary and find lots of other examples. With older pupils, look at phrases that work as palindromes, for instance 'a man a plan a canal panama'.

● Think about the abbreviations used in text messages. Examine the way that homophones are used, particularly those provided by numbers. For example, 4 (four) taking the place of 'for' and 8 (eight) providing the 'ate' sound in words such as 'great'.

● Play a game of 'Countdown'. Invite a volunteer to pick cards with a selection of vowels and consonants. Challenge the pupils to make the longest word possible, or to create as many different words as they can.

You Can... Think about strategies for spelling

As they move up the school, your pupils will hopefully become comfortable with the spelling of basic words. They will begin to encounter a range of more complex vocabulary and they will need to develop strategies for spelling these new words.

Thinking points

● As adults, we often use strategies for spelling in a subconscious way, barely thinking about what we are doing. Our role as teachers is to make these techniques explicit for our pupils.

● Encouraging your children to think through the problems they encounter and how these can be solved, will help them to become more independent learners.

● Some words will be relatively easy to spell, because they conform to the rules of English pronunciation. Those words with irregular spellings will need to be remembered or learned by sight.

● Unusual, active approaches to the learning of spellings will be more memorable and engaging for your class.

Tips, ideas and activities

● Identify the words that cause your children the most difficulty and work as a class to devise ways of overcoming the problems. For example, you could:
  ○ List some hard to spell words; ones that the children typically get wrong. To do this, they could look through each other's exercise books and make a list of commonly misspelled vocabulary.
  ○ Think about why some words are hard to spell and which bits of the word are often spelt wrong. For example, where there is a 'hidden' sound, as in 'February', children will often miss out the 'r' because it is not heard.
  ○ Work as a whole class to create memorable strategies for remembering problem words. For example, saying 'February' over and over again, voicing and emphasising the hidden sound to make it easier to remember.
  ○ Create huge displays of some problem words so that they are easily visible on your classroom wall. For example, printing them out one letter to a page on a computer and sticking the letters together to create a giant word.

● When introducing a new topic, give the children a 'bank' of technical words that are hard to spell. Print these onto individual 'word cards' for the pupils to use during the topic.

● Have a 'word of the week', focusing during the week on lots of different approaches for getting problem words right. For example:
  ○ Kinaesthetic exercises, such as modelling a word in clay or with pipe cleaners.
  ○ Visual activities, such as painting the word or making collages.
  ○ Sensory exercises, involving taste, touch or smell; making textured pictures of a word, or creating a word using raisins or sweets.

● Choose some simple words and ask your children to make a list of more complex ones that arise out of these, for example:
  ○ out: outing, outer, outrage, outside, outsider, outward
  ○ create: creation, creative, creator
  ○ miss: missing, missile, missive, mission.

You Can... Create and analyse characters

Exploring how an imaginary character feels will help your children develop the skill of empathetic thinking. Pupils can also use fictional people to help them think through tricky emotional and social issues.

Thinking points

● The characters that young children create are often fairly flat and one-dimensional. Developing more complex characters will require the use of higher-order thinking skills, such as reasoning and lateral thinking.

● Drama-based approaches to characterisation allow your pupils to 'experience' how it feels to be someone else in a different situation.

● Analysing the characters created by other authors will help your children develop their own writing skills.

● Imaginary characters offer a safe way of exploring thoughts and feelings that children might find difficult to express.

Tips, ideas and activities

● Explore a range of imaginative and unusual ways of creating a new character. For example, you could:
   ◦ use images from magazines to make up an identikit character, with different body parts stuck together to create the whole
   ◦ show the class a handbag; examine the contents and talk about the type of person who owns this bag
   ◦ place a set of clothing on the floor, including a hat and some shoes; think with your pupils about the character who left the clothing behind
   ◦ get hold of some puppets and ask the children to voice the different characters.

● Use drama to examine familiar characters and to explore their motivations and emotions. For example, you could:
   ◦ use a chat show format to interview a character
   ◦ hot seat a range of people from the same book
   ◦ create frozen images to sum up a character.

● Try this 'thought tracking' exercise to help your children examine a character's thoughts and feelings.
   ◦ Use an open space, such as a hall or gym. Divide the class into pairs.
   ◦ Arrange the children standing in two lines, opposite their partners, down the centre of the room. They should face inwards, leaving enough space so that someone can walk between the lines without knocking into anyone.
   ◦ Ask a volunteer to play a character from a familiar story.

● Identify a point in the story where the character faces a challenge or is in a particular emotional state. For example, Theseus in the maze, about to face the Minotaur.
   ◦ The child playing the character walks between the two lines. As he or she passes, the others whisper what they imagine the character is thinking. For example: *scared, fearful, I can hear roars, what if the Minotaur eats me?*
   ◦ Repeat the exercise with other volunteers taking a turn.
   ◦ Talk with the class about the experience and how it felt to 'hear' the character's thoughts.

You Can... **Explore what we read**

Once we have learned how to decode individual words, we can then move on to getting meaning from different pieces of text. Thinking about how their brains extract meaning from text will help your children develop the skill of metacognition.

Thinking points

● When children first learn to read they will sound out individual letters and letter blends to make sense of the words. From this first stage of reading out loud, they move on to sound out the words silently, in their heads.

● Most of the words in an average piece of writing are only there to help the text make sense and to flow. In the previous sentence, the key words include *most, words, average, only, help* and *make sense*.

● It is possible to read without the need to sound out the individual words. We can skim our eyes over a piece of text and still gather meaning from it, without sounding out the individual words.

● Learning to skim read will help your children read faster; it will also aid them in note-taking and revision.

Tips, ideas and activities

● Use the photocopiable sheet on page 59 ('How does reading work?'). After completing the exercises on the sheet, ask the children to think about what happened in their brains as they read the extracts. With the second extract, a very interesting effect sometimes happens; the reader *thinks* the text is actually written correctly, even though it is not. Our brains help it appear to make sense; on closer inspection the words are actually written in the wrong order.

● Arrange your children sitting in pairs, facing each other, with one book between each pair. Ask one child to hold the book, and the other child to read it to his or her partner upside down. After the pupils have tried this activity, invite them to talk about what happened in their brains as they read.

● Teach your children some speed reading techniques. Use the following exercises to show them how much faster their reading can be.

  ● Give each child a piece of text face down, something with technical words in it, for example from a science or geography book.

  ● Ask the pupils not to look at the text until you say 'Go'.

  ● Set a very short time limit, about ten seconds. When you say 'Go', the children turn over the text and see how much information they can gather in this brief time limit.

  ● Turn the text face down again and quiz the pupils about its content. Talk about what they did to extract meaning.

  ● Now give a slightly longer time (about 30 seconds) and ask the children to skim through the piece, finding out what it is about. Ask them to try and avoid 'sounding out' the words in their heads. Again, turn the page over and talk about the text.

  ● Finally, ask each child to highlight the key words in the text passage. Working as a whole class, find out which words were highlighted and why.

You Can... **Analyse how stories begin**

Looking closely at stories generates lots of opportunities for developing thinking. A writer can capture our attention and interest in the very first paragraph of a story, by making effective use of language and situations.

Thinking points

● Analytical exercises can help us explore how stories work. In the best stories the technique will be hidden; use close study to help your pupils see the underlying structures and techniques.

● Thinking about and understanding the techniques used in fiction will help your pupils write better stories of their own.

● This type of activity will often particularly appeal to boys; it demonstrates the need for technique as well as imagination in a story.

Tips, ideas and activities

● Use the photocopiable sheet on page 60 ('Openings'). Guide the children through the analytical exercises below.

● Allocate each 'opening' a score from one to ten, to describe how gripping it is. Ask your pupils to justify their scores, picking out examples from the text to consolidate their thinking.

● Using a highlighter pen, ask your pupils to mark different features of the text: words or phrases that they find particularly interesting, or examples of repetition.

● Identify some specific language features with the class; ones that have an impact on the levels of tension in the text. Encourage your children to think about how these features work on them as readers. Introduce the terminology for any new language devices. Here are some examples of features to explore:

  ◦ Personification – 'The land below seemed to tremble', 'the threat of the coming rain'. This feature helps to give more depth to the text and a background sense that something terrible is coming.

  ◦ Questions, listing in threes – 'How did he get here? Where was the train going? And what would be...?' The use of questions helps involve the reader. Listing in threes gives a rhythm and urgency to the text.

  ◦ Story questions – '... at least that was what I thought at first'. A story question puts a puzzle in the reader's mind and sets him or her thinking about what might happen later on in the story.

  ◦ Questioning/exclamatory dialogue – 'What do you want from me?', 'Help! Somebody help!' This dialogue makes the scene feel vivid and tense.

● Do a writing activity arising from your study of these texts. Ask your pupils to:

  ◦ choose their favourite opening and write a continuation of the story

  ◦ choose their least favourite opening and write a review of the imagined book from which it comes

  ◦ write one additional sentence for each opening

  ◦ decide on a title for each story.

You Can... **Communicate in mathematical language**

Maths is a great subject for developing critical thinking. Your children will need to use thinking skills such as logic and reasoning in order to solve problems and find accurate solutions.

Thinking points

● Maths has a 'language' all of its own. This language is made up of numbers, shapes, words for giving directions, time and so on.

● Many of the terms that we use in maths will also be familiar from our everyday lives. Understanding the link between maths and real life will help your children see the relevance of the subject.

● Mathematical language needs to be used in a precise and accurate way. The picture activity described on this page will help your children understand why this is important.

Tips, ideas and activities

● Use the photocopiable sheet on page 61 ('Maths picture') for an exercise in using precise mathematical language.

● Ensure that the class are familiar with the terminology needed to describe the picture. This will include: small, medium, large, right, left, top, bottom, circle, multiplication, division, percentage, octagon, rectangle, oblong, triangle, equilateral, isosceles.

● Divide the class into pairs.

● Ask for one volunteer from each pair. Give these children a copy of the 'Maths picture' sheet. Explain that they should keep it hidden from their partners.

● The children with the pictures must describe it to their partners, using the correct mathematical terminology. The partners must draw the picture as accurately as possible from this spoken description.

● The pupils describing the picture must not use hand signals or correct their partners. The pupils drawing the picture can only ask questions requiring yes or no answers, for example, 'Is it bigger than this?'

● When the pictures are completed, the children should see how well they have done.

● Bring the class back together to talk about the mental processes involved in describing and drawing the image. Identify the need for accurate language and detailed description.

● You might like to give a prize for the pair who complete the activity most successfully.

● Talk about the use of mathematical language in our everyday lives. Ask a volunteer to describe the journey from home to school. The rest of the class should raise a hand every time they hear a mathematical word, for example 'right', 'left', 'up', 'down' and so on.

● Take your class into an open space such as a hall or gym. Create an obstacle course using tables, chairs, cones and so on. Divide the class into pairs, with one child acting as guide and the other closing his or her eyes to be guided. The children have to navigate their partners through the course, using mathematical terminology.

You Can... Think about food and digestion

Looking at food and digestion offers some great opportunities for practical and fun experiments. It also encourages your children to think about what they eat and whether they have a healthy diet.

Thinking points

● It is a sad fact that some of our pupils do not have a particularly healthy diet. This, combined with a lack of exercise, can lead to problems with both mental and physical health.

● A poor diet can lead to short-term problems, such as difficulty in focusing or poor behaviour. It can also lead to longer term, more serious health issues, such as heart disease and diabetes.

● Research has shown that many children are dehydrated and this can have a negative impact on their concentration in lessons. Some schools now allow pupils to have a water bottle with them in the classroom.

● Encouraging your children to think about a balanced diet will hopefully give them the information they need to make better, healthier choices.

Tips, ideas and activities

● Create and display life-sized body shapes. Ask the pupils to draw around each other on large sheets of paper. Label faces, hair, teeth, nails and so on, as well as internal parts, such as stomach and intestines.

● Think about a varied and healthy diet. Divide the pupils into groups, one each for:

- carbohydrates
- proteins
- fruit and vegetables
- fibre.
- fats
- vitamins and minerals
- water

● Ask each group to research their food type and its importance for a healthy body. Invite them to present a short summary to the class.

● Bring in your 'shopping'; carrier bags containing different foods and drinks, including processed and unprocessed foods.

- Show the items one at a time.
- Ask the pupils to verbally 'fight' for those that fit into their category. (Some foods will 'belong' in several groups.)
- Encourage them to use reasoned statements saying why they 'own' a food. For example, the vitamins and minerals group might say, 'We should get the oranges because they contain high amounts of Vitamin C.'
- Vote to decide where each item should go.
- Think about how balanced your shopping was.

● Use this exercise to explore digestion. You will need:

- two clear plastic bags, one small, one large
- two lengths of hollow soft plastic tubing, one small, one large
- some hard and soft foods, such as a banana and a cracker.

● Demonstrate the path of food through the body, using pupil volunteers.

- Put the foods into the small plastic bag (the 'mouth').
- Use fingers (the 'teeth') to crush them.
- Cut a hole in the bag and attach the small tube. Push the food through the pipe (the 'oesophagus').
- Attach the large plastic bag (the 'stomach'). Squeeze the food into the stomach and churn it up.
- Add the large tube (the 'intestine') and squeeze the food through.
- Plop the waste into a bowl!

You Can... **Think about ways of communicating**

ICT is a great subject for developing thinking. When they use new technologies, your children will employ critical thinking skills such as reasoning and logic. They will also use creative thinking to express their ideas, solve problems and so on.

Thinking points

● Recent innovations in ICT, particularly email and the internet, have caused radical changes in the ways that we communicate with each other.

● There is an immediacy with these forms of communication that can be very useful. However, we must also take care to be thoughtful about what we read and write.

● Finding the appropriate form and tone with which to communicate will require your pupils to think carefully. They will need to consider the audience for their ICT and how this might affect the way they express themselves.

● The project on this page asks the children to use a combination of both critical and creative thinking skills. It also encourages them to communicate with a range of different audiences.

Tips, ideas and activities

● Set your pupils the challenge of planning, creating and marketing a new drink product, using lots of different ICT skills to communicate with different kinds of audiences. Here are some suggested activities.

  ● Bring in a wide range of sizes and shapes of bottles, containing all kinds of liquids, from water to face cream.

  ● Look at each type and ask your pupils to think about the messages each container gives. Study the labels to see what information they include and to consider the designs.

  ● Focus more specifically on drinks containers. Gather a selection together and ask your children to look at the product names, drink colours, actual contents and so on.

  ● Think about the way that many drinks' companies link their products to images of energy, sport and health. Talk with your class about the reality; that sugary drinks give them a burst of energy, but this is short-lived.

  ● Find websites for the different drinks companies, by doing a search on Google. Use email to communicate with some of these companies, for example asking for information or some samples. Discuss with your pupils the appropriate format and language to use in their messages. One useful website address is www.britishsoft drinks.com.

  ● Encourage your children to interview other pupils across the school, to discover what kind of drinks they like and how often these are consumed. Organise this information into a spreadsheet.

  ● Ask your pupils to create their new drink product, using various software programmes. They will need to: design a bottle, name the drink, decide on the contents and create a label.

  ● Explain that they will need to devise a promotional strategy for their new drink. Ask them to use a range of advertising media, for example: designing a poster, creating a web page, recording a radio jingle, creating a magazine advertisement, or devising a commercial for television.

You Can... Use water as a topic for thinking

Thinking around the subject of water can raise some interesting philosophical questions, as well as developing a variety of geographical skills.

Thinking points

● Water plays a key part in our everyday lives; it is so ubiquitous that much of the time we might overlook how important it is.

● In developing parts of the world, getting clean drinking water is vital for survival. In richer countries, water has become something we can use for pleasurable reasons too.

● Human beings have found many uses for water, beyond the necessity of using it to quench our thirst. We use it for transport, for leisure, for making energy and in many other ways.

Tips, ideas and activities

● Undertake some general work around the topic of water.
  ○ Discuss how we use water. Consider vital uses (such as drinking, washing) and unimportant ones (such as leisure, watering the garden).
  ○ Create a mind map of water-related words, both natural and manmade, for example: *rain*, *storm*, *hail*, *drain*, *gutter*, *umbrella* and so on.
  ○ Use circle time for some water associations. Begin with a word (for example, *sea*, *wash*) and ask the children to think of related words around the circle.
  ○ Talk about how water moves and the words we use to describe it: *flow*, *pour*, *splash* and so on. Encourage your children to use their bodies to illustrate different types of movement.

● Pose some philosophical water-related questions for your children to discuss.
  ○ Who 'owns' water: in rivers, in the sea, when it falls as rain?
  ○ Why is it wrong to waste water?
  ○ In a world where some people die for lack of water, can it ever be right to use it for pleasure (swimming pools, garden irrigation)?

● Look at water in the context of the weather. You could:
  ○ Study, photograph and draw the patterns made by frost on different surfaces, on a cold winter morning.
  ○ Create crystals in a freezer, using different types of liquids and look at the results under a microscope.
  ○ Collect rainfall over the course of a school year, displaying the information you gather on a graph or bar chart.
  ○ Ask your pupils to present a weather forecast to the class, creating symbols to show the different types of weather and sticking these on a map of the UK.
  ○ Use a large world map and add sun/rain symbols to show different weather patterns around the world.
  ○ Get your children to lie on their backs on a grassy area in the playground, to study and draw different cloud formations.

● Encourage your children to use their sense of smell to examine samples of water: tap water, mineral water, rainfall, pond water, water from a swimming pool and so on. Use blindfolds to heighten the experience.

You Can... **Use artefacts to stimulate thinking**

Children find objects such as historical artefacts very inspiring in the classroom. Anything that is not normally seen in a school environment can stimulate some extremely interesting thinking.

Thinking points

● Artefacts from fairly recent history should be reasonably easy to get hold of. Approach older grandparents for items from the time of the Second World War, such as ration books and coupons.

● Older artefacts can be harder to find; you may find some realistic replicas in the shop attached to a local museum. Alternatively, the museum may be willing to lend you a few genuine objects to show the children.

● Hiding artefacts will add a sense of realism and will make your children curious to find out more.

Tips, ideas and activities

● Digging up objects from the ground will really engage your children with the process of historical discovery. You can use this activity to get your pupils thinking about how we discover more about the past. You might find that the experience turns some of them into budding archaeologists!

  ● Find an area of soil or grass outside where you are allowed to dig.
  ● Hide some artefacts, such as old coins or flints, in this area. Bury them reasonably deeply and in layers so that the 'older' objects are lower down.
  ● Alternatively, for a more genuine (although probably less exciting) experience, simply choose a spot to dig in and see what is there!
  ● Explain to the children that they are going to undertake an archaeological investigation. Explain relevant health and safety issues.
  ● Before you begin, ask the pupils to think carefully about the equipment they will need and how they should go about their investigation.
  ● Collect the necessary equipment: garden trowels and forks, compost sieves, plastic trays for holding objects, string and canes for marking out the search areas, squared paper for marking down finds.
  ● You could watch some extracts from television programmes such as *Time Team* to explore how an archaeological dig works.
  ● Once you have dug up your artefacts, bring them back into the classroom. Ask the children to think about what these objects are 'telling' them.
  ● Encourage them to use logic and reason to construct their answers, but also to include some lateral, creative thinking as well.

● In a similar way, you could use other ways of 'hiding' artefacts to inspire your children and excite their curiosity. For example:
  ● some 'treasure' in an old-looking chest
  ● some documents in an envelope marked 'Top Secret: Do Not Open'
  ● creating a time capsule with your class to bury in the school grounds.

You Can... **Invent a new product**

Taking a new product from initial conception to final design is a very satisfying experience. The process involves many types of thinking skills, particularly reasoning, analysis, creative and lateral thinking.

Thinking points

● As a subject, design and technology uses an interesting mix of different types of thinking. The pupils have to be innovative and imaginative to devise new ideas; they also have to use logical and critical thinking to bring these ideas to fruition.

● Where the children work on a product that is familiar to them, such as a new game or toy, they will be able to bring their own prior experiences to bear.

● It is useful to get your pupils to create a product that can be tested out in a 'real life' situation. The ideal market for testing their product is the other pupils in your school.

Tips, ideas and activities

● Use the 'role of the expert' to plan and make a new product. The children take on the role of product developers for a toy manufacturer, creating a new board game. They must work through the various stages of product development, including:

  ● research
  ● prototypes
  ● final product
  ● planning
  ● market testing
  ● advertising.

● During the research stage you could:

  ● Ask the pupils to consider the potential markets for board games, thinking about how toy manufacturers appeal to different age groups.
  ● Arrange a visit to a toy shop, to analyse the competition. Look at where the games are displayed; those at eye level on the shelves are the big sellers. Take notes on how much each game costs.
  ● Alternatively, bring in some sample games to show the class. Include 'classics' such as Monopoly, Trivial Pursuit, 'Snakes and ladders', draughts and chess. Play the games and think about how they work.
  ● Ask the children to think about what makes these particular games so appealing; Why have they outlasted others to become childhood classics?

● During the planning stage you could:

  ● Consider the range of possible 'topics' for games: those that test knowledge, games of chance, games with counters and so on.
  ● Split the class into groups to think of ideas. Encourage the children to gather lots of potential ideas before narrowing down their thinking.
  ● Think about and cost the materials that they will need for their games, including dice, cards, boards and so on.

● Now encourage the children to develop a first stage product; a prototype that they can test. You could do this by taking the children into other classes to demonstrate and test their games on other pupils.

● The pupils should make any necessary changes to their game, as a result of this testing. They can now devise a finished product.

● Analyse how games companies advertise their products. Look at advertisements in a range of media: television, magazines, radio, billboards and so on.

You Can... **Think about visual and tactile elements**

Children love to experiment with different materials, particularly those with interesting colours or fascinating textures. The chance for an active, 'hands on' experience in art lessons can be really engaging for your pupils.

Thinking points

● Art is a great subject for those children who like to learn in a visual or kinaesthetic way. Even those with limited ability in the traditional, academic subjects can gain a feeling of success.

● Art can also offer a way for children to express their thoughts and feelings in a personal and individual way.

● There are lots of links between work on visual and tactile elements in art and other subject areas, for example, science and creative writing.

Tips, ideas and activities

● Use blindfolds to stimulate thinking about the tactile properties of different materials. As they touch different objects, ask the children to talk about the sensations they feel and the associations they make.

● Gather lots of types of cloth, perhaps from a charity shop or from a recycling centre. Work as a class to create a patchwork blanket that utilises different textural qualities.

● Visit your local DIY store and collect colour charts for paint. Ask your pupils to think about:
  ○ the kind of moods that different colours create
  ○ where these colours are seen in everyday life (such as in a landscape, in buildings, in clothing and so on)
  ○ how they can recreate similar colours in the classroom
  ○ which colours are 'warm', and which ones 'cool'; why this is? What effect do warm/cold colours have on mood?

● Use a colour wheel to show your children how different colours link. Talk about which colours work well in combination; those next to each other on the wheel and also those directly opposite each other.

● Look at visual and tactile elements in the natural world. You could:
  ○ bring in flowers with different coloured and shaped petals
  ○ find leaves with interesting textures – prickly, soft, furry, crinkly and so on
  ○ feel different kinds of stones: gravel, pebbles, rocks, both rough and smooth
  ○ explore the ways that water and light can interact on a sunny day.

● Use an ICT session to create lots of different kinds of lines. Ask your children to:
  ○ Open a Word document.
  ○ Display the 'Draw' toolbar; go to 'View', 'Toolbars' and click on 'Drawing'.
  ○ Create a page of different lines; go to 'Autoshapes' on the 'Draw' toolbar, then click on 'Lines' to choose a style of line.
  ○ Double click on the line to make changes to the colour, style and weight, or to add dashes.

You Can... **Use language to inspire dance**

Inspiration for dance can come from many sources: from music, from art, and also from language. The written word has been used by many great choreographers as a stimulus or backdrop for their work.

Thinking points
● Words and dance movements might seem to be very different forms of expression. However, they can both use a symbolic language as a way of expressing an artistic sensibility.

● Thinking of ways to express words through movement will help your children widen their vocabulary in both English and dance.

● Linking words and dance shows your pupils how language can be given a sense of movement. This should hopefully help your more able pupils add pace and interest to their writing.

Tips, ideas and activities
● Use different kinds of words, particularly adjectives and adverbs, to inspire your children. For example:
  - directions: in, out, up, down, over, under, through, between, around, across
  - opposites: black/white, open/closed, happy/sad, yes/no, fat/thin
  - speeds: fast, slow, quick, sluggish, swift, leisurely
  - ways of moving: slide, jump, skid, turn, hop, run, saunter, stretch, bend
  - textures: rough, smooth, sharp, bumpy, shiny.
● Create letter shapes as a starting point for dances, encouraging your children to use their arms, legs, heads and bodies to 'draw' letters in the air. Choose fluid shapes such as S, M and O for flowing movements and more linear letters such as T and Z for jagged ones.
● Experiment with some onomatopoeic words, finding ways to express them through movement. For example:
  - crash
  - bang
  - miaow
  - woof
  - boo.
● Create a mind map of words connected to animals, thinking particularly about the way that different animals move. For example:
  - cat: sleek, slinky, pounce
  - elephant: plod, heavy, trunk
  - snake: slide, slimy, slither
  - bee: buzz, fly, sting.
● Use a range of texts as a stimulus for movement work: poems, stories, newspaper articles, myths and fairy tales.
● Discuss some traditional stories that have been used for ballets. Play your children extracts of music from these ballets. For example:
  - Peter and the Wolf
  - The Nutcracker
  - Coppelia
  - The Sleeping Beauty.

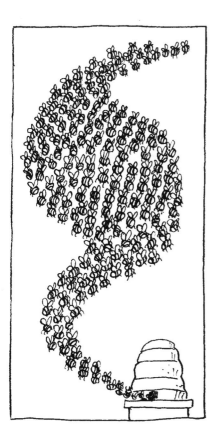

You Can... **Experiment with sound and noise**

Experimenting with different ways of making sounds is a lot of fun. By using some lateral thinking your children should be able to come up with lots of unusual and imaginative sounds.

Thinking points

● We might tend to think of 'music' as being about a melody created by instruments, but music can be much more than this, for example: percussion, the sounds made by our bodies, the absence of noise that is silence and so on.

● Thinking about sounds will help your children become more aware of the effects of noise on their emotions and moods. This should encourage them to think about how the noise they make can have a positive or negative impact.

● The typical classroom is filled with noise throughout the day. Periods of silence can have a wonderfully calming effect on children's behaviour and can really help create a good atmosphere for learning.

Tips, ideas and activities

● Create a list of all the different things in the classroom that can be used to make a sound. This could include:
  ● desks and chairs
  ● resources (such as building blocks, pens)
  ● parts of the building (such as walls, windows)
  ● their voices and bodies.
● Try this 'sound-tracking' exercise to explore how sound can create a strong sense of place.
  ● Find an open space, either a classroom with the furniture cleared to the sides, or a hall or gym.
  ● Ask the children to lie down on their backs in a circle, with their heads at the centre and feet outwards.
  ● Give the class a setting, for example: a rain forest, a prison, a ship at sea, a Victorian classroom.
  ● You could add some other elements to create more interest, for example timing (at dawn, at sunset) or weather (a storm).
  ● Ask the pupils to create a soundtrack of the location. To do this, they should make vocal sounds using either noises or words.
  ● Encourage the class to give a 'shape' to the soundtrack; to start quietly, rise to a climax and then gradually fade out.
● Ask the class to recreate manmade sounds, considering how these noises affect us. For example, types of:
  ● transport (cars, trains, aeroplanes)
  ● machines (robots, production lines)
  ● clocks (ticking, alarms).
● Think about the absence of sound and how this makes us feel. Introduce the class to the work *4'33"* by avant-garde American composer John Cage, which is made up of four minutes and thirty three seconds of silence. Talk about:
  ● whether this can be classed as a piece of music and why/why not
  ● how the audience might have reacted on first 'hearing' this piece
  ● what point John Cage might have been trying to make.
● Create percussion using a range of recyclable and rubbish-related items, banging on dustbin lids, shaking plastic bottles filled with different materials and so on.

You Can... **Look for links between religions**

Finding links and connections is a key thinking skill. The ability to look for what is similar, and why, will help your pupils find patterns in their lives, the world and people around them.

Thinking points

● We live in a world where religious beliefs are sometimes used as a method of separation between different people. As a result it is ever-more important that we show our children how similar many faiths are in what their followers believe.

● It is fascinating to explore the connections between religions, both from the West and from the East. This exploration can throw up some very interesting thinking about how and why religious beliefs have developed.

Tips, ideas and activities

● Use the photocopiable sheet on page 62 ('I believe'). To do this exercise, the children will need to know about or research the religions listed in the National Curriculum. These are Christianity, Buddhism, Hinduism, Islam, Judaism and Sikhism.
● To complete the activity:
  ○ Read through the sheet with your class.
  ○ Ask the pupils to think about how and why many faiths are linked.
  ○ Provide access to materials to use for research.
  ○ Instruct the children to write in the names of all the religions for which each statement is true.
● The BBC website has a very useful series of pages on different religions, giving details of the history, customs, beliefs, worship and holy days of major faiths. See www.bbc.co.uk/religion/religions/
● Explore the similarities between religious festivals in different faiths. Look at the symbolism that is common to many religious celebrations, thinking about what these symbols might mean and why they have been adopted. For example:
  ○ light: candles, fireworks, bonfires
  ○ food: special foods, sweets, fasting
  ○ colours with special symbolic meanings
  ○ songs, music and special dances.
● Ask your children to think about the idea of community and how people can belong to both a local community and also a religious one. Encourage them to consider how people of different faiths might be bound together by a common moral code.

Eyewitness account

An eyewitness is a person who sees something happen. An eyewitness describes what he or she saw after the event.

● The police will interview an eyewitness to find out more about a crime that has taken place.

● An eyewitness account from history can tell us more about events that happened many years ago.

Eyewitness accounts are not always completely accurate. Try this exercise to see how good you are at observing an event.

1. Give a description of the person who came into your classroom. Include information about his/her hair colour, hair style, clothing, height, build and so on.

_____

_____

_____

_____

_____

2. Write an account of what the person did when he/she came into your room. Include as many details as you can.

_____

_____

_____

_____

The senses

When one of our senses is taken away, our other senses have to work much harder. Blindfold your partner and test each of his/her senses. Write down your findings below.

1. Hearing

What do you think it is?

_____

_____

What does it make you think of?

_____

_____

_____

_____

2. Touch

What do you think it is?

_____

_____

What does it make you think of?

_____

_____

_____

_____

3. Taste

What do you think it is?

_____

_____

What does it make you think of?

_____

_____

_____

_____

4. Smell

What do you think it is?

_____

_____

What does it make you think of?

_____

_____

_____

_____

Chain of consequences

Our actions have consequences; sometimes good, sometimes bad.

1. Fill in the blanks to create a logical chain of consequences.

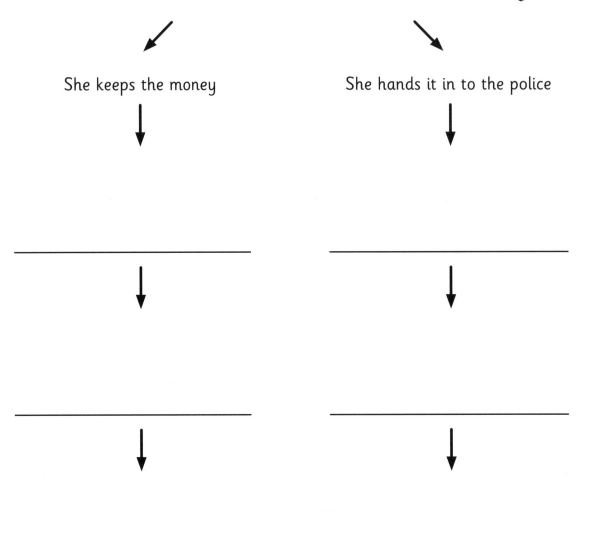

Emily finds a bundle of £20 notes in the street.

She keeps the money   She hands it in to the police

_____   _____

_____   _____

2. Now create some more chains of your own.
   Here are some ideas to get you started.

- Jack is offered a cigarette by a friend.
- A gang of bullies tell Amir to give them his money.
- Rebecca sees a friend stealing from the teacher's bag.
- James spills paint on his sister's new dress.

How does reading work?

The way that our brains work when we read is really interesting. We can still make sense of writing even if:

● it is spelt wrongly
● the letters of the words are mixed up
● the words are in the wrong order
● there is no punctuation.

1. Read this text and write it out correctly.

We cna stil red a peace of wirting evan wehn the wrods r seplt rongly adn awl mixxed up.

_____

_____

_____

_____

2. Do know you this what piece writing of says? If do you, it write below.

_____

_____

_____

3. there are no full stops commas or question marks in this piece of writing can you still read it how do you think your brain does this isn't that clever

_____

_____

_____

_____

Openings

1. The train thundered along the rails, moving ever faster as it picked up speed. In the sky, heavy clouds bubbled up ominously. The land below seemed to tremble

against the threat of the coming rain. The scene outside flew past the windows so fast that Jack couldn't make sense of it. How did he get here? Where was the train going? And what would be waiting for him when it arrived?

2. It was a very ordinary Monday, at least that was what I thought at first. Maybe I woke up slightly later than normal, but apart from that it was just the same as every day that had gone before. My first clue that something weird might be happening was when I went down for breakfast. Mum, dad, my big brother Toby, all sat silently at the table, waiting for me. Now that was a bit unusual for a start.

3. "What do you want from me?" she screamed, as she backed up against the hard, cold wall.

The creature paused for a moment as though puzzled, then continued its forward motion. Its injured leg scraped along the ground, oozing a trail of stinking green slime. Emily spun wildly from side to side, looking desperately for an escape route.

"Help! Somebody help!" she screamed again. No answer. There was no one left to answer. There was no one left to save her.

Maths picture

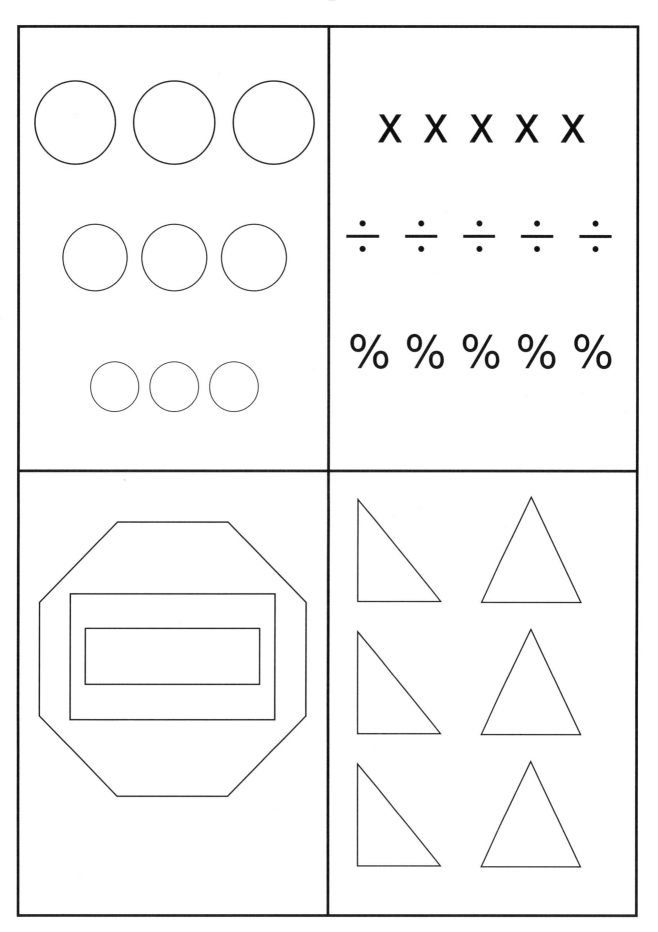

I believe

There are lots of different religions in the world. Each faith has its own special beliefs and customs, but there are also a lot of links between the different religions.

Your task:
- Read through the statements below.
- Decide which statements apply to which religions. Choose from: Christianity, Buddhism, Hinduism, Islam, Judaism and Sikhism.
- Do some research to find the answers. You could use books or the internet; you could interview people belonging to different faiths.
- Write the correct religion below each statement.

My religion was founded by one special person

_____

_____

I worship in a special building

_____

_____

My religion has a sacred book

_____

_____

I use prayer to speak with my god

_____

_____

Index